WILD SPIRIT FIRE

WILD SPIRIT FIRE

FREEDOM FROM FEAR AND SEPARATION

Danielle Kort

Copyright © 2023 by Danielle Kort

Cover design by Danielle Kort

All rights reserved. This book or any portion thereof may not be reproduced or used in any manner whatsoever without the express written permission of the publisher except for the use of brief quotations in articles and book reviews.

ISBN-13: 978-1-958848-90-6 print edition
ISBN-13: 978-1-958848-91-3 e-book edition

DreamSculpt Books and Media
An imprint of:

Waterside Productions

Waterside Productions
2055 Oxford Ave
Cardiff, CA 92007
www.waterside.com

DEDICATION

This book is dedicated to my mother, who now serves as an angelic presence in my life.

DESCATES

TABLE OF CONTENTS

Acknowledgments · ix
About the Author · xi
Preface · xiii

Chapter 1—The Nightmare of Separation · 1
Chapter 2—Dissolving Density · 16
Chapter 3—Breathing Peace · 30
Chapter 4—Whispers from Within · 44
Chapter 5—Dedication to Awakening · 57
Chapter 6—Tears of Gratitude · 67
Chapter 7—Bursts of Joy · 80
Chapter 8—Wild in Wonderment · 90
Chapter 9—Sacred Sovereignty · 100
Chapter 10—Soul Embodiment · 113
Chapter 11—Conscious Creation · 126
Chapter 12—The Dream of Unity · 139

ACKNOWLEDGMENTS

Mom: You introduced me to spirituality and you set me on my path. The day you transitioned out of physical form was possibly the hardest day of my life. Thank you for your assistance with writing this book and from your now higher perspective, helping me remember that we are one. PS Purple looks so good on you!

Dad: I'm so very grateful for you and your insurmountable generosity in helping bring this book to life. Thank you for believing in me.

Jared: Thank you for showing me the ropes and being spacious enough to allow my true voice to emerge.

Kyle: Thank you for your love and support, not only while I brought this creation to life, but in all the five beautiful years we spent together. I will cherish you forever.

Amara: A large reason why I was able to express this written word is because of you and your profound trainings. Thank you!

Lisa: You reminded me that I could slow down and return to my own natural rhythms. Had I rushed, this version of the book would not have had the gestation time needed to be birthed. Much gratitude!

ABOUT THE AUTHOR

Danielle Kort is a New Earth Ascension Guide dedicated to ushering consciousness into a new era, where all beings recognize the divinity within them. As an intuitive channel for the higher realms, she brings forth wisdom teachings to assist those willing and ready to move into expanded states of awareness. Through channeled courses, retreats, and one-on-one sessions, Danielle guides her clients to clarify their higher purpose and embody their creative genius in alignment with the divine design of their energetic signature. She holds the blueprint for 5D leadership and in her work, she grounds in the vision for a collective of individuals who are true to themselves and sovereign in their choices. With a decade of experience leading others to channel their life force energy into soulful creations, she has raised the bar for what it means to lead a wildly spirited life.

For more information visit:
www.daniellekort.com
Instagram.com/danielle.kort
Facebook.com/ascensionguidedaniellekort

PREFACE

This book took shape through a series of channeling sessions I did from December 2020 through August 2022. When I channel, I open my energy channels to receive higher divine wisdom from a source we are all connected to and ultimately one with. The way this looks for me is that I sit in a comfortable position and work with a medicinal Amazonian herbal blend called rapé (pronounced "ha-peh" or "rapay"), which supports me in opening my energy channels and dropping into a deep meditative state with ease and speed. Rapé is used by indigenous peoples ceremonially in the form of prayer to induce visions and gain clarity, to call upon the supportive forces of nature and animals of the forest, and to bring about healing, energy, and strength.

Rapé is administered with a ceremonial pipe called a Kuripe, which I gently place against my mouth and nostril. After setting my intention, I blow the Amazonian snuff through my nostril, where it moves up into the nasal cavity and does its magic. I do this with each nostril and then sit in silence until I hear words through clairaudience. Then I record the messages, which I later transcribe. Channeling has always been a big interest of mine. I took an introductory course on channeling many years ago, but I am mostly self taught through practice.

You might wonder how I know what or whom I am connecting with as I open myself to channel these messages. First, I use intention, and through this intention, I call upon and bring forth information from God Source Consciousness, my Higher Self, my true primary spirit guides, and those benevolent beings who walk in light and come from a unified perspective. Second, through significant amounts of inner work, I've cleared programming, conditioning patterns, and trauma so that I am a clear channel for the highest wisdom to flow through my being.

DANIELLE KORT

The contents of this book serve as a transmission of higher consciousness, so as you read the words, I suggest receiving the messages into your heart and being rather than only using logic to figure it out. Allow this book to transform you in the ways it is designed to, knowing that logic can help you understand the concepts better, while opening your mind and your heart to receive this transmission of light can expand you beyond your current vibrational set point.

CHAPTER 1—THE NIGHTMARE OF SEPARATION

There exists a magnificent force of energy, so brilliant and so bright, it weaves through every being, every particle, through all things. It makes up All That Is. This light emanates from inside your core. You can feel it when you tune in to your breath, letting all of your outer worldly attachments and burdens go. In essence, it is what you are.

You came into this incarnation with the intention of exploring consciousness in a different way. So you focused your awareness into a single, individual expression. And voilà! Here you are, emanating your light in the form of a human being. As a young child born into the world, you spread this light freely. While you may have had patterns of resistance carried over from other lifetimes or existences, you were aware, at least on some level, that you are a divine extension of Source Consciousness.

You played and created with an untamed imagination, and you laughed in wonderment with this fun, new physical experience. Of course, along your trail you were bound to pick up on energetics and dynamics that were less than harmonic. These expressions became habits, and these habits became ways of life, ways of interacting with your world. These disharmonic expressions came from ways you learned to perceive. You learned to perceive by picking up on the cues of your parents or caretakers, your school teachers, your peers, and the media or information you were taught to tune in to.

That brilliant light within you became dim, overlaid with limiting perception, causing you to believe that experience itself is punishing you for being sinful or bad—that you must live up to a certain societal measurement or you won't be acceptable or lovable; that the material world is an absolute truth and we all must agree on one "correct" way to go about things. Meanwhile, you forgot that you occupy multiple dimensions of consciousness and have access to unlimited possibilities from which you can choose. You forgot that the purity of your inner light is your true nature, and your spiritual lineage became buried underneath a falsified world of materialistic and mind-based aspirations.

Yet there was no mistake in any of this, as you were seeded with a divine design created for your soul's evolution here. To incarnate into the collective consciousness of this planet, you agreed, prior to being born, that you would undergo a massive process of forgetfulness. You came here knowing that you are an eternal being of light and one with All That Is. You knew that you are infinitely loved, adored, and cherished, and that you are an unconditional lover. You knew that you *are* love. There was no question about this.

Yet as you focused your awareness into this little peephole, you would come to find a new experience awaiting you. This experience would challenge you in every way. You would face unconscious, fear-based realities as you explored the vast number of experiences "out there." What you were being challenged with, what you *are* being challenged with, is to reunite with that brilliant spark within you and to use that light to find your way home.

Coming Home to Your True Self

Home is not some location "out there" that you are trying to get to; it is within you. Coming home is returning to your true nature. It is the feeling you get when perhaps you have previously felt lost or far from this inner dwelling of yours. We return home after we have journeyed through consciousness and we have reconciled what had been lost or forgotten regarding our true, eternal essence.

To return home is to reside in total peace. When you decided to make the pilgrimage into this physical incarnation, it was done so with great joy and purpose. Even though you knew inevitably that you would encounter experiences of pain and suffering, you knew you would grow immensely through these experiences. What you may not have known is that this pain or suffering, dis-ease or disharmony only comes from your perception.

For a long period, the collective consciousness ventured off into unconscious realities, where perception becomes muddied and misconstrued. When you focus your awareness through a lens that is unclear, that is unconscious, you are tuning in to a reality that can feel heavy, depressing, painful. If this is what the majority of those around you are tuning in to, you can either agree to participate in this kind of world or you can begin to expand beyond it. Your Higher Self designed a curriculum for your soul's evolution here. By rediscovering your sovereignty in perception, you can eventually graduate from your unconscious experiences.

The unconsciousness is the forgetful veils you agreed to go under in order to be part of this physical experience. The veils are not meant to last, however, and this is why you are awakening to your true essence now. You are remembering why you came here and what your soul's purpose was in doing so. As you steered your focused awareness into this individual expression, you came under the illusion that you were separate from the whole. Rather than singing and dancing in joyful exuberance that you're having this orgasmic, unique experience in the physical, you likely got caught up in unconscious and limiting beliefs about yourself and the world around you.

The Illusion of Separation

One of the root beliefs that limits your creative capacities and aligns you to realities that feel dull or fearful is the belief that you are separate from God Source Consciousness and Creation itself. When you believe you are separate from the pure divine light within you (your true nature), you are conflicted inside of yourself. You are in a constant fight for your survival. You feel lonely, lost, misunderstood, unloved, unworthy. You mistake your physical body for being all that you are. You believe you must compete for scarce resources, and love seems to evade you at every turn. You are surrounded by billions of people in the world, but somehow you feel *so alone*.

Separation is experienced in the body as a resistance to the flow of life force energy or the Spirit of Creation. It causes you to feel deeply at odds with your experience. This is where fearful thoughts and heavy emotions are formed. When you believe this is the only experience available to you, it can become difficult to find inspiration and a reason to live. Yet this is where you are challenged to see beyond the illusion; to open your eyes to greater possibilities than you've previously known. It takes courage and strength to face the unconsciousness that you agreed to wade through, to explore. Yet as you open your eyes and choose to remember your connection and oneness with All That Is, the inspiration and joy that flows into your experience is profound.

Separation is a consciousness or belief system that you can opt out of as you grow your awareness of it, realizing it was an illusion all along. When we forget that we are connected to and one with God Source Consciousness/the Universe/Divinity, we form identities that do not represent or embody the truth of our soul. In doing this, our soul fragments, becoming wrapped in these ego identities. Because these parts of us lose touch with their divine essence, they cannot find their beneficial purpose or place in the universe, causing us to feel lost and insignificant. This is a normal part of the exploratory process you signed up for. Yet, as one who is awakening to their true, divine origins, you now have the opportunity to reclaim those soul aspects and reunite them with their greater whole.

For example, you might feel torn when making a decision because a part of you feels one way while another part feels a different way. By observing these inner voices, you can use your discernment to determine which are identities born of separation and what is the voice of your soul. Shining the light of your awareness on that which is not your greater truth or your Whole-ly truth allows these old programs, beliefs, and identities to fall away. We practice gaining greater awareness through self-observation. By observing your ego thoughts, patterns, and habits with divine neutrality or non-judgment, you become aware of them, and in time, they cease to exist inside of you. Aspects of your soul essence that had been wrapped up in these identities are then freed, and you reclaim them into the kiln of your soul light.

It Was All a Dream

When you go to bed at night, you enter a sleep state called dreaming. Our dreams are interpretations of our innermost thoughts and beliefs. As we grow in consciousness, these beliefs can conflict with our newfound understandings. These conflicts can be fearful in nature, and this is why you might say that you had a "nightmare." Our dreams present us with our fears, ego fantasies, and karmic patterns, but we can override these if we choose.

By choosing love instead of fear, by choosing our higher truths over our conditioned beliefs during our sleep state, we relinquish the need to play out these realities in our waking state or physical experience.

Our waking state is a dream in itself, and just like our sleep state, this physical reality is formed from our innermost beliefs, whether they're conscious or unconscious. Our waking nightmare takes hold or occurs when the beliefs we have about ourselves and the world are detrimental to our well-being. When our beliefs stem from fear, victimhood, shame, unworthiness, greed, materialism, or addiction, for example, we carry these heavy burdens, we thicken the veils of illusion, we dim our light, and we create our own nightmare. Your nightmare, or what we'll label a nightmare, is comprised of disharmonic thoughts, emotions, and situations that deal with yourself, your relationships, your finances, your career, your health, or any aspect of your life. Our beliefs are created in many ways and can originate from our meaning-making, past life experiences, other existences, or inherited from our ancestors.

Inheriting Ancestral Beliefs

Let's say your mother yelled at you as a child for breaking her flower vase. The experience really shook you up, and you harbored an emotional upset within you. Even though it was an accident, you took your mother's reaction to mean that you are a wrecking ball and cannot be trusted. The upset is centered around this story that you created, and these kinds of stories become your beliefs. These disempowering stories or storylines can play out throughout your physical experience and often across many lifetimes.

These stories or storylines can also be handed down to you through your ancestral lineage, like hand-me-downs that don't fit the true you. You fall heir to them and adopt them because you think you have to, because you don't realize you have other options, limitless possibilities, in fact. These hand-me-down stories or beliefs are often sewn from the same fabric of personal and collective trauma that your ancestors experienced.

Imagine a grandfather who has lived through a time of war. He experienced lots of unrest and faced the unfathomable—seeing his family members being killed before his eyes. This can cause post-traumatic stress disorder

(PTSD) or emotional trauma within his consciousness. If you ask him about the world, he might tell you that others cannot be trusted, that you must watch out for your enemies, that there are threats around every corner. And this feels valid for him because of what he has experienced in his life. Whether or not he tells you about his experiences verbally, these emotional traumas and beliefs are passed down to you genetically, vibrationally, if they were not tended to by this ancestor or the succeeding generation. If you claim these beliefs as your own, if you don't tend to these emotional traumas with the love of your Spirit, you will replay them in *your* life's story.

You can also take on beliefs created and agreed upon by a society, civilization, or collective. You might see these storylines or beliefs in advertisements, the movies, hear them over the airwaves, or simply pick up on them through collective thought. You might latch on to these ideas because you want to fit in and be accepted. Yet ultimately, if the belief or narrative doesn't fit or align with who you truly are and you still hold on to it, you are sequestering yourself to an experience of pain and sometimes lifetimes of pain. This pain is a prison cell of your own making, separating you from a sovereign and harmonious reality.

It is rather nightmarish to believe that we can be controlled by another's mandates, structures, or systems that don't have our best interest at heart. You might feel like a character in a horror movie if you walk to your car at night in fear that someone will jump out and attack you. It is not a dreamy experience to dislike your body, your looks, or your life because you compare it to some idealized image in the media. These kinds of beliefs become programmed in our subconscious minds and cause us to fear others and hate ourselves. Here is where we lose touch with the thread that weaves us together and allows us to prosper and thrive as a family of light.

Awakening from Separation Consciousness

Separation consciousness can feel like a nightmare, and yet it is an experience that has ultimately helped us grow. It doesn't need to be judged or hated or resented. It's simply something you can awaken from, something that you *are* awakening from now. Feel into the relief that bubbles up inside you as you realize it was only a nightmare; that the fears and monsters of a separation-based belief system were only illusions of a programmed mind, and you can change your mind as easily as you can change a television station. If you want to take any possible perceived drama out of it, which the word nightmare could stir up, you can bring it into neutrality by saying it was only an experience. The word nightmare is used just for an understanding, to decipher the difference in feeling between living in separation consciousness and living an embodied experience of Unity Consciousness and Oneness. One feels dense, heavy, burdensome, icky, traumatic, and the other feels light, effervescent, connective, loving, fun, free, joyful.

So while you might say that one felt like a nightmare or nightmarish in certain moments, it doesn't mean that in all moments as a sleepwalker you were feeling that way. Feel into your life's experience. Can you sense when you did, at times, experience that loving connection, the warmth of your soul shining forth? You'll probably find that you've had moments or chunks of your life where you could sense the light of your soul more predominantly than other times.

Bringing your conscious awareness to those places inside of you that have been gripping onto your nightmare is when true empowerment blossoms. With that awareness, you shine light on those places within and help free those soul aspects of yourself that have been focused upon a separation-based perspective. You help to integrate these aspects back into Oneness.

That difference in going from the heavy, upsetting, burdensome perspective to this more enlightening, joyful disposition is really a celebration. It's a freeing experience that you can be extremely appreciative of. To be walking the walk, embarking on this sacred journey and discovering the purpose of having gone on this journey of awakening, is exhilarating.

In walking our soul's path, we are tasked with surrendering all that we are not and embracing and embodying all that we truly are on a moment-by-moment basis. In doing this, we ascend or expand in consciousness. When we let go of identities that were only created for a temporary experience, we make room for higher universal truths to emerge. Not only are we integrating those soul aspects, which had become wrapped in ego identities, but we are also integrating our higher dimensional aspects, which are already attuned to Unity Consciousness. Expanding our consciousness to embrace our multidimensionality is perplexing to the ego, or the one who has forgotten, but required for our soul's evolution here.

DANIELLE KORT

Integrating the Light

Integration is the process by which we assimilate higher light quotients into our body and beingness, which then projects into our outer reality. Our soul is made of light, and as we shine this light on identities and constructs, which were only created for a temporary experience, they dissolve. This makes more space for our soul to emerge. The more you tune in to and honor your soul, the more light you will integrate. As you bring each of your soul aspects back into conscious awareness and wholeness, you shine brighter and brighter.

Light is a high vibrational frequency, so as you activate, integrate, and radiate your light, your vibrational frequency rises. When your frequency is higher, you feel lighter, brighter, and more vibrant and joyful. You feel a closer heart connection with others and are more turned on by your interests and passions. In a lower frequency, you feel heavy, dull, and confused. You might feel like nothing is working in your favor and hopeless about your path or your life. You can feel or read vibrational frequency by utilizing your intuitive gifts. For instance, you might see a preview for a horror movie and get a heavy feeling in your gut, or you might watch a litter of puppies snuggling and feel light-hearted and warm inside.

Ascension: Becoming Conduits for Divine Light

Ascension is the process of clearing out all of our separation-based identities and belief systems, activating and holding more light, and returning to our pure, unified nature within a higher realm of consciousness. We are conduits for divine light, and as we allow ourselves to fully receive it into our being, we are reunited with our inner Creator. Our creative capacities grow and become enhanced as we awaken and integrate the light of our soul. Every time we rise in vibration, we ascend a little more. We rise as we let go of anything that no longer serves a purpose and make room for that creative life force energy, that wholly light to flow through us freely. As we emanate this light, we are no longer encumbered by false ideologies or expectations of the ego. We are free to create from the pure joy and love within us.

For a purposeful amount of time, we are unconscious, not present to all the possibilities that surround us, not present to our true, multidimensional nature. Yet this is what we are each awakening to now, each in our own divine timing. As we relax and surrender to our higher consciousness, we open a portal to new worlds of exploration, first within us and then in the outer reflections of our life's experience. As we return to the present moment and consciously choose our higher, most natural expression, we align with a more heavenly experience for ourselves. We are here to remember our mastery as the powerful creators we have always been but had simply forgotten. The difference between a sleepwalker and a conscious creator is that the conscious creator no longer disconnects from the light that shines from within her.

When we act from the unconscious places inside of us, we tend to do things on autopilot. We react from fear or habit rather than observing and deliberately responding to what's unfolding before us. We don't use our creative powers in an intentional way, often because we have forgotten that we have creative choice in the first place.

Opening Up to Multidimensionality

Imagine standing in line at a cafeteria waiting to get a bowl of the same old bland soup you've been served every single day. Because this has been your experience since the first time you stepped into this cafeteria, you expect nothing different. You go through the motions like a robot performing its programmed tasks. One day, however, a spark of inspiration hits you. The words "look up" come into your consciousness. So you look up, and behind the checkout counter you see a door that's slightly cracked open.

You sense you're not really supposed to go back there, but you can't help but be magnetized to whatever is behind that door. So while the cook isn't looking, you follow the inspiration to sneak back there. You open that door a bit wider, and you almost can't believe what's laid out in front of you: a huge buffet with a sizable variety of delicious-looking foods. A stack of freshly washed plates and a tray of silverware is waiting for you to use. The buffet was there all along; it just took a moment of deeper awareness to be open to divine inspiration and to courageously act on it. Then you were able to expand into a whole new possibility for yourself.

Whether consciously or unconsciously, what we believe becomes real in our life's dream. What we agree to or allow shows up for us. It is a freewill universe, after all. Free will means we get to choose how to direct our will, and when we direct it toward mundane, fearful, or nightmare-like realities, then that is what we are shaking hands with and agreeing to dream more of.

In truth, it all exists. All the experiences you could ever dream of. So if you choose to continue opting into your nightmare of separation, then you continue to experience it. By acting from this separated place within you, you are tuning in to your separated nightmare experiences "out there." By warring with your neighbor, by condemning those with opposing beliefs, by trying to conquer Mother Nature, by battling with the different aspects of yourself, you continue your nightmare.

Dissolving Your Fears

When you engage with your fears as if they're big scary monsters, whether fighting them or running from them, you make them real. They chase you through halls and up trees. They have you stuttering on stage while everyone laughs at you. They sleep with your husband. They force you to bend to their command. But again, our fears are only as real as we make them; no more, no less. As we focus on our fears, believing in them, they become real in our experience. As we give our power to our fears, they grow bigger and create more separation inside of us.

It is in raising our conscious awareness to meet that of our soul's perspective that we can view our fears in a new light. We do this by returning to presence, by opening our hearts and remembering that we are safe. We must choose presence over our fear perspectives. When we return to presence, we can face our fears with the divine love inside of us. Our love is greater than any fear we had created in moments of unconsciousness or a belief in separation. When we step back, away from fearful thoughts or situations that appear frightening, we grow spacious, and our capacity to meet the fears with love, with acceptance, with compassion is enhanced. Suddenly, what once felt overbearing or all-consuming now appears infinitesimal, like a gnat that you simply swat away.

If you believe in separation, then you draw to you life circumstances that confirm this belief. Your beliefs focus your energy, and where you direct your focus is what you call to you as your outer world experiences. When you are unaware of your thoughts, they become unconscious beliefs, making it difficult to attract what you truly want or desire.

Have you ever lain in bed awake, filled with anxiety, imagining fear-based scenarios that might happen the next day or sometime in the future? Then, did you revisit those same fear-based scenarios with that same dread-filled energy? Perhaps weeks or even years later, this exact scenario, which you had feared and contemplated, now manifests as a physical experience for you to confront. When this happens, are you really that surprised? Maybe you say to yourself, *Dang, I knew this would happen!* It is through our focus, whether it be on what we fear or what our heart truly desires, that our experience is shaped and created.

You may only be realizing this now, but you are an infinitely powerful creator. This is only scary to the part of you that has learned to distrust yourself, to distrust your higher innate wisdom. Inside your nightmare, you gave fear more power than you gave that eternal light within you. Fear was a creation born of separation consciousness. It has played a role in your human experience and has taught you a lot. When you are presented with fearful reflections, it causes you to dig deeper and return to the love of your Spirit. You have grown through this process. You have become more valiant in your choices to show up in love, as love.

Facing your fears head-on ignites a fiery passion for aiding and assisting others in expanding beyond their limits as well. It is a delicious experience to go beyond your limitations. You can feel the extraordinary power behind you as you do this. When you move through your fears, you are greeted on the other side of it with higher, lighter, and brighter reflections, realities.

It is only when we allow our unconscious realities born of fear to run us, to drive us, that we continue our nightmare of separation. We have the choice as to what we believe. So the questions you can ask yourself are: Will I believe the thoughts born of fear? Born of a belief in separation? Or will I return to this present moment where all is well, where all is one?

Fear is not something our Highest Self experiences or perceives. How you perceive is how you experience. When you let go of your fears or you face them head-on, moving beyond them, you open a portal to higher love and greater freedom. You begin to exist in the safety inside your heart. You have always been safe. It was only in exploring your unconscious realms that you veered away from this remembrance.

In signing up for this ascension journey, you knew you would be required to face each challenging experience with a higher understanding than you've previously had by reuniting with the divine love inside of you. No matter how big or scary that monster would appear to be, you knew that you could always lean into the undying love and support here for you in this present moment. When we can catch our automatic, knee-jerk reactions—those moments when we go back into the unconscious fears—and we can meet them with our loving awareness, we can soothe and dismantle our emotional traumas and limiting beliefs. The more you choose presence, the more you vibrate with the frequency of love and with the heartbeat of All That Is.

The Dream of Your Spirit

That larger, eternal, all-encompassing version of you has always been here. Let go of those thoughts that became beliefs that told you otherwise. Rub your eyes and open your spiritual sight, as you were always meant for a heavenly and dreamlike experience of life. All that you have known yourself to be, born of unconscious beliefs, is ready to fall away now, and what remains is your pure essence, your peaceful heart, your brilliant and higher mind.

As you radiate this most exquisite expression, you light the way for others. You create at the top of your genius. You dance like no one is watching. You serve through your fiery passions. You work and play in collaboration with your Spirit, as your Spirit, and in unison with All That Is.

As you return to presence, you learn to focus on "The Dream," the dream you are choosing to line up with and embody, the dream of your Spirit; not the fantasy of your ego—that's different. The fantasy of your ego can often lead you to believe that you will experience this heavenly dream, but when that fantasy materializes, you can easily see that although it seemed so promising, the roots of intention behind that fantasy were based in separation consciousness. There is still the fear perspective running the show.

In your ego fantasies, you will not find that soul fulfillment you truly want to experience. You may find temporary happiness, some satisfaction, but nothing lasting. The ego fantasy is based in separation, and it's different from the dream of your Spirit. The dream of your Spirit fits like this uniquely beautiful quilt piece into the collective dream woven by unity.

The Dream of Unity Consciousness

To embody Unity Consciousness is to be in flow with the Spirit of Creation, to be attuned to the harmonics of a higher octave, where peace pervades and love is the underlying intention behind all action and nonaction. To reside in Unity Consciousness means to remember that we are extensions of, and ultimately one with, God Source Consciousness and all of Creation. To be unified as a collective does not mean that we must think, feel, or do the same as everyone around us. It means that we radiate as exquisitely unique expressions of the Divine in a harmonious and honoring manner. As a divine spark of God Consciousness, you incarnated here to experience the contrast and grow through the challenges that would inevitably present themselves. Yet ultimately, you have always carried the dream of unity within your heart, and this guides your choices so that one day you might realize this dream in full color.

We are dreaming all the time. This human experience has us dreaming, whether we're sleeping or awake. When we dream unconsciously, on autopilot, reacting to what we see and reinforcing "what has been" as our only choice, we continue this nightmare of separation. This is simply because the collective has been hanging out in the unconscious realms. It's what we have been participating in, unknowingly. Yet, as a sovereign being of light, this can change with your own conscious, creative choice to awaken into a new dream altogether.

While it might appear that all things are separate—me from you, sky from ocean, humans from nature, God from creation—there is a unified consciousness underlying the world of form. Even in those darkest moments when you feel completely alone, there is an energetic field connecting you to every other living being in creation, beyond what you see physically. This energy spans out from your heart and links to all other hearts, creating our collective experience. Through this field, we can send messages, healing intentions, and comfort to others, which can be felt regardless of the physical distance between us. This web is called the unified field, and you can access it with presence and pure intention. As we raise our consciousness, we merge with this field of unlimited energy and unbounded awareness.

We affirm our nightmare when we judge ourselves and others, when we believe we are powerless or victim to circumstance, when we see the one before us as an enemy. Here, we see through a distorted lens of perception, and we stifle our creative possibilities. We can drop that lens of separation by letting go of our nightmarish thoughts, beliefs, and stories, by seeing it all for what it was—just a temporary experience. Then we awaken to the truth that we are eternal beings not created from lack or limitation or bound to any set of rules, systems, physical identities, or personas.

We awaken to the truth that we are free, always have been free and always will be. We awaken to the fact that sovereignty is our birthright, that no one and no-thing can control us. We awaken to our creative capacities and laugh in wonderment when we realize just how much we played a role in creating our experiences. This ends up bringing us the empowerment we've always been seeking.

As we opt out of our temporary experience based in separation consciousness, we are able to sit in this ever-present energy of divine love. We can free ourselves from the monkey mind and whatever had us running in circles to acquire physical possessions or secure safety or prove our worth. We're able to rest in that unconditional awareness that *all is well;* that nothing outside of us is needed because this present moment is more than enough and is all there is. These realizations, these experiences of coming back to your true self, are what heal the traumas and dissolve the nightmares. And more and more, you will find yourself existing from this state of pure presence.

The striving and grasping, which stemmed from your separated mind, fall away and feel like a distant memory, like a drama or thriller you once watched that no longer affects you. Find this place of stillness, this wellspring of well-being, and come to it often; drink from it often. Even if it's only once a month to start, then eventually once a week, then once a day, and then moment by moment, as you allow this new state of consciousness to emanate from your core and envelop others in love, healing, and empowerment.

As you embody your dream and this dream of a unified consciousness, you radiate that out and anchor this new perception, this new way of being and doing, into collective awareness. That remembering ripples out into the planet and into the universe. Everything shifts and changes around you, affecting those among you in the most glorious ways.

As you begin to recognize where you have unconsciously cut yourself off from that brilliant light within you, which connects you to the unified field, to all other beings, to God Source Consciousness, you will discover the Divinity that you are truly made of. Not only will you come to know cognitively that you are an expression of the Divine, that you are supported immensely and infinitely, but you will begin to embody this remembering. The feeling of being separated from your multidimensional expression has served its purpose in strengthening your conviction to shine your loving light. This light is the torch you are here to carry through the darkness, through the unconsciousness, and it will lead you back home to your true, eternal nature as one with all of creation.

CHAPTER 2—DISSOLVING DENSITY

While the surface you're sitting on may appear solid, in truth, everything is made up of energy—color, matter, sound, you name it. Energy is a vibrational frequency, and frequencies have many different qualities that provide us with a magnificent variety of sensations and experiences. Whatever frequencies we hold within us or resonate with at any given time serve a purpose along our path of awakening. As we become aware of what we're ready to shed, we are gifted with the opportunity to let the old, dense energies go and make room for the new, higher vibrational energies to integrate within our field.

Realizing Yourself through Densities

A density is a space of consciousness or plane that you tune in to by way of your vibrational frequency and your level of awareness. Densities themselves are frequency; they are within you and are projected out as a physical environment with which you can participate and interact. They are designed for our learning and growth and serve as a creational playground for your soul. You might compare densities to grade levels in school. Once you have demonstrated your ability to master a certain density, you graduate or ascend to the next level of understanding.

At this time, the human collective is making its way from the third to the fifth-density earth plane, which we call Gaia. Although it is a collective goal, each individual being completes this journey in their own divine timing. In third density, we form ego identities, where we perceive as separate individuals and tend to view our world as purely physical. Belief systems we form and adopt from this collective level of understanding and carry over from past or other existences tend to become rigid and polarized. We see in terms of black or white, right or wrong, us versus them, and we can feel quite alone or separate from our Source and those around us. Here, we have the opportunity to remember the truth of our light and to love and receive love even when faced with that which challenges our true nature.

As we awaken, we become aware of the 3D matrix system we have been participating in. We see its limitations, and we sense that there's got to be more than this. We vacillate between our mind and our heart, which are saying opposing things. Duality manifests as conflict within us, and as we move into 4D, we are challenged to merge, unify, and harmonize this inner conflict. We are met with the opportunity to find our own inner truths beyond what we have been taught. Here, we expand beyond the "little me" where we felt victimized and lost in survival-based mentalities. We stop trying to derive happiness and peace from Maya, the illusion (from other people, experiences, or substances), as now we realize that our true nature *is* one of peace, love, and joy and that we can radiate this from within.

In third density, the ego identity unconsciously moves toward separation. In the fourth density, the awakening being works toward unity, detaching from duality and transcending lower densities. The higher or more expanded self unifies with All That Is and moves in flow with all of Creation.

It is in 5D where we live and love unconditionally. We have let go of all attachments and judgments and primarily exist within a space of divine neutrality. Here, we no longer take things personally, as we have let go of the person we once thought we were. In 5D, we accept all expressions, viewpoints, and choices of ourselves and others while upholding sacred boundaries of self love and love for all. To come into wholeness, we extend compassion to all parts of us and all other beings, remembering that we are each a divine extension of Source Consciousness. We acknowledge and honor ourselves and others in our wholeness, and we accept our brothers and sisters even when they are expressing fear and separation.

This ascension journey that we are embarking on is both a collective and individual experience. We focus, however, on our own inner journey of consciousness expansion since everything exists within us. As we reach higher levels of awareness, we remember other existences and bring forward the gifts and abilities we embody in these other lifetimes. Speaking in terms of densities as higher or lower does not mean that any are right or wrong, better or worse than another. Densities have to do with a bandwidth of vibrational frequencies, and as you integrate and hold more light your vibrational bandwidth grows, and you expand your awareness into new, higher density planes of existence.

As we vibrate at higher frequencies, we align with realities that respond to those frequencies from within us, which means more harmonious and heaven-like realities emerge. Raising your vibrational frequency and expanding your consciousness is a process you get to participate in, and even initiate, as you become aware of the inner workings of this evolutionary journey. Understanding that our bodies and energetic fields are going through a complete transformation is a great starting point. It is paramount that we love, nurture, and nourish ourselves throughout this process.

As we ascend in consciousness, we embody our soul or Higher Self more and more. By activating and integrating the light of your soul, old stored dense energies are kicked up and are forced to shift or be pushed out of the way to make room for this new light coming into your field. These densities can be cellular memories, beliefs, emotions, traumas, or information that are held within your body or aura.

As you purge density out of your energetic field and physical body, you become lighter and you rise in frequency. You might see this as a detox that must take effect. In the world of health and wellness, one knows that this is an important phase of ridding the body of toxins. You may feel the urge to vomit, have a bowel movement, or blow snot from your nose when this higher vibrational light enters your being. That which is exiting your body is simply where the densities were being stored. While this can be a confronting or uncomfortable process, when we allow the energies to move out of us with an attitude of gratitude, thanking them for how they have served us, we pass this density with greater ease. It is of great value to be kind and gentle with ourselves during this transitionary time, similar to how we might treat ourselves when recovering from an illness.

Density serves us for a purposeful yet temporary experience, one where our creational process is slowed down so we may learn to choose consciously and intentionally. Imagine thinking about and feeling the sensation of being inside a hot air ballon, and then instantaneously, you're twenty thousand feet in the sky actually going on a hot air ballon ride. Then imagine the fear of falling out of this hot air balloon overtaking you and the dread of plummeting to your death, and manifesting that a moment later. Density acts like training wheels so that we can master our creative abilities by allowing us to practice at a slower pace.

As we work through the realms of lower density, we tend to imprint this density with our unconscious fears, emotional traumas, and limiting beliefs. In awakening and becoming aware of the dense energies that no longer serve us, we are granted the opportunity to let them go. Anything out of alignment with our soul expression carries a lower vibrational frequency, creates density inside us, and reflects in our outer world. If something in our experience is creating separation and dissonance rather than serving to unify or harmonize, it is density.

We can surrender and allow density to move through and out of us with grace and cooperation. It is the ego that strives to maintain control and resists this transformative process. Take notice when you find yourself judging or holding back from allowing these dense emotional, mental, and physical energies from expressing and exiting your being. Surrender, at least in this context, is not a weakness but a gift we give ourselves, which opens us to greater harmony and bliss.

Everything Must Go

We transmit our physical reality through the vibrational frequencies we hold within us. If we are holding on to old, outdated beliefs and habits so we can feel safe and avoid the unknown, for instance, then we are missing the opportunity to align with new magnificent realities in a higher octave or on these higher density planes. The density within us, including old limiting beliefs and lower vibrational emotions, must be surrendered. Like a yard sale, "Everything must go!"

Anything seeded from the old consciousness or unconsciousness is dense vibrational energy and is ready to leave your experience as soon as you're ready to let it go. Fear, separation, disrespect of self and others, the belief in lack of anything, including love, integrity, resources, time—these are all density. By freeing these old stored densities, we gain easier access to an unlimited source of pure divine light and become greater conduits for this energy.

Purging the densities of the lower realms activates our light body. The light body is where our Higher Self, or soul, eventually resides. As this energy body activates, it creates temporary imbalances while dense energies move out and new, higher light quotients move in. While it might feel like you're sick or that something is wrong and needs to be fixed, it is simply your physical body trying to tune to higher frequencies. You might want to run to a doctor and take medications to fix what seems broken, but this only suppresses and impedes the inevitable, which is that a beautiful transformation is underway. While the ego tries to hold on and fix, the soul assists in this transformation, helping the body purge and move the old, dense energies out to make space for the new.

Rising in Love

To dissolve density, we choose to vibrate within the divine frequency of love rather than the heavy, dense frequency of fear. Culturally, our definition of love is far from accurate, as we tend to make love small and superficial. "I will love my child because she is behaving well." This is not the divine frequency of love, and while we might think of it as "conditional love," in truth, it is not love at all. It is an aspect of ego attempting to control or dictate a person, outcome, or environment. "I'm in love with my new shoes." These statements create a distortion that we only label or identify as love.

Ultimately, love is spacious, and fear is confined. Fear creates more fear; love creates more love. Love is ever-present and is what you truly are. After becoming so familiar with the frequency of fear from years of suppressing your authentic expression for fear of being judged, doing what others told you to do for fear of getting in trouble, or staying in a job you hate for fear that you can't find anything better, choosing love is a courageous act. Because we had become so entrained in the frequency of fear, it takes all our presence and conscious choice to move back into the frequency of love. As we set down the constructs, mandates, and beliefs created from fear, and we shine our loving light, our vibration rises, our perception shifts, and it becomes easier and easier to remember that love is, and always has been, our true nature.

Imagine walking on a path with a slight incline that eventually leads up a mountain. You consider this a low-risk hike on a well-marked trail. You've packed a gigantic backpack with everything you believe you'll need for this journey. You have a reason for every item you packed; generally, it's because these belongings make you feel safe and comfortable. Primarily, though, you brought these things because you've owned them your entire life, and they're just what you're used to having with you.

Along this trail there are tiny offshoot paths marked "fear" and "love." You can choose to continue on the love path, which takes you up the mountain, or you can choose the fear path, which takes you back down the mountain. These crossroads appear nearly every five feet on each path. Every time you decide to choose the love path, you are required to remove a small item from your backpack and leave it behind. Little do you know that these items each represent density and they only weigh you down. As you choose the path (or frequency) of love in those little, everyday choices, you lighten your load and make it easier and more enjoyable to continue along your path of love. You rise in frequency, little by little, as you move up these slight inclines.

Now, this is a frequently accessed hiking trail, and while it doesn't mean you won't gain elevation, it's for beginners and will take you a while to make it up to higher planes of density or consciousness. Now, let's say one day you come to a crossroads where you are presented with the opportunity to make a bigger choice. The love path now turns into more of a rock climbing or mountaineering trail rather than a hiking trail. The slope is steep and feels like the Wild West, uncharted territory, the path less traveled. Here, the fear path looks quite inviting. You look up, however, and you can see that once you're at the top, you'll have a really awesome view.

Although this love route looks more difficult, it actually isn't. The real difficulty you will face is in choosing the love route over the fear route. The fear path might be tempting because it seems so much easier. Attachment to your old baggage is the only other thing that can hold you back now. To take this steeper love route, you are asked to open your backpack and leave behind a bigger item—a habit, pattern, construct, belief, or reality that you've been carrying.

Once you make your choice and part ways with this item, all there is to do is to trust your Spirit or Higher Self to reach down, lend a helping hand, and guide you up the rock. No safety rope or gear is required, as there is no risk in choosing this higher vibrational frequency of divine love. The more you trust, the smoother and more effortless this ascent will be. You may feel some fear or doubt at first, but what matters is that you're choosing the path of love, regardless.

Once you've made it up to this new level of awareness, you look out from this higher vantage point, and you tear up because you are so touched by the absolutely breathtaking view (or reality). Your heart flutters as you become present to all the other fresh, mind-blowing possibilities now available to you. You are deeply grateful for what this experience has left you with: true soul fulfillment plus more courage and confidence to choose divine love again and again.

Removing Your Armor

In third density or lower realities of perception, we often see our world as rigid, solid, and unchangeable. From this vantage point, it can be hard to believe in the miraculous because it feels like nothing can be transformed. All you can see is what has already been created. Here, you will unconsciously hide from yourself and lie to yourself and others in order to survive in a scary and threatening world. This is what anchors you to denser reflections.

In higher, lighter, or more expanded places of perception, your physicality becomes more transparent, more translucent, and realities become more flexible and bendable. You no longer hide your true self or your true intentions. You remember that you are inherently innocent, and you remain true to yourself and others in all moments.

Here you know that being open, honest, and transparent creates a safe world, and so you act on it. You take full responsibility for your thoughts, words, and actions, so you flow with the lighter, brighter vibrational frequencies aligned with your soul's perspective, your Higher Self's vantage point. Eventually, the inner conflicts recede, because you're no longer resisting your life's unfolding or fighting with those before you. All the parts of you, all the versions of you, merge with the unified field, and you move in harmony, in sync with the heartbeat of the universe. Synchronicities, magic, and miracles now become a part of your everyday life.

Picture yourself walking out the door and the sun gently kissing your forehead. You get into your car, turn on the radio, and your favorite song is playing. An image of a friend's face comes into your awareness, and two seconds later, that very same friend calls you. Or perhaps one afternoon you feel the urge within to go to the park and you flow with that inspiration. Once there, you strike up a conversation with a stranger who happens to mention something that ends up being the final puzzle piece you need to bring your vision to life. This is what it feels like to live in coherence with your true essence, to flow with Creation itself.

To flow is to move like water: lightly, freely, fluidly. When we bend ourselves like a pretzel, conforming to meet the expectations of society or hiding our true colors for fear of rejection, we dam up that flow of energy. That energy is the Spirit of Creation, which animates us when we stay true to ourselves. Growing up, we learned to hide our true selves behind false identities and masks. We built walls to protect our hearts because we were afraid—scared we were not enough, terrified we would get hurt again, worried that we were unworthy. This weighed us down in dense, unconscious realities.

It was in these spaces that we were asleep. Was it bad or wrong to sleep? No, it was simply a part of our human experience, and it was built into our life's design to eventually awaken, to emerge from that deep slumber. We knew that eventually we would notice all the weight we'd been carrying around and chuckle to ourselves about how silly it is to try to be something we are not.

Imagine a knight donned in chain mail, an armored body suit, a shield, and a sword. He is preparing for battle, to joust against his opponent. But after years of fighting to protect his name, his dignity, his kingdom, he grows weary of the resistance within him. He looks out his window and sees the sun shining brightly on the meadow of wildflowers and gets a glimpse of a different possibility, of a different kind of world. Perhaps he is able to feel into this world and what it would be like to live in peace, in harmony, with a pure heart and a calm mind. If he opens the door and he's prepared for battle, then this is the reality he walks into. But if he can surrender his belief in a fearful and dangerous world, he will open that door to a new world altogether. So the question then becomes, What world would you like to participate in? There are endless possibilities to choose from.

We can remove the armor we've been wearing out of fear, but first, we must become *aware* of that armor. We can exhaust ourselves to the point of surrender, and this works as it needs to. We can also take a step back from our busy lives and see what is weighing us down, what is no longer true for us, where we are spending excessive amounts of energy trying to be good enough, look good in the eyes of others, or hide from the changes we know we need to make. If we surrender these things starting now, we save ourselves from loads of work later. We opt out of needing to learn the hard way. You do not need to be the knight in shining armor; what you want to do is shine so brightly that the armor melts away.

There are many people who would like to believe that density is created by things outside of themselves, but this is a victim perspective. Once you realize that you have placed each obstacle, person, and circumstance on your path in order to grow, that is when empowerment becomes your new way of life. Density is something you may hold on to because of the belief that what has been is all there is or that your world is absolute, solid, and separate, void of interconnectivity or greater possibility. This fixed lens through which most people see their world can keep them locked into identities such as feeling powerless or victimized by their circumstances. Your experience of life is relative to how you perceive, to what you understand, and to what you believe, moment by moment. When we can ease our grip on those painful and limiting ways of perceiving, we can begin to let them unravel and dissolve.

You are so much greater than your circumstances, as your circumstances are your own creations, and creations are fluid, changeable, and transformable. You are not stuck with any belief, and you can transform your world through intention and focus. Is your focus on what's *not* working? Is it on what proves your story right that you cannot be, do, or have whatever your heart desires? Then this is what you are calling to you in the form of your outer world reflections. To dissolve the density, we must go within. We shift our focus to our inner world, letting go of anything that's not in resonance with what and who we truly are.

Feeding Your Body in Light: Initiating Light Activations

In our purest state, we are the frequency of light. To return to this state of grace, we feed ourselves in light. Light is anything that supports us in embodying Unity Consciousness and our true nature. The beauty in integrating more light is that we get to shine brighter, and our radiance acts as a catalyst for others to shine their inner light as well.

One way you can introduce more light into your being is by exposing yourself to direct sunlight and holding the intention to receive and absorb the sun's light codes. These codes reawaken your twelve-strand DNA and activate your light body. Breathe these solar rays into your being, imagining your inner light growing as you do this. The sun may appear to be outside of you, but this is only a mirrored reflection of what's within you. Meditate on this ancient understanding to fully embody and assimilate your light. You are an eternal Spirit cloaked in physicality, a light being growing in her radiance.

Whatever comes from nature or organic origins holds a higher or lighter frequency. Things that are inorganic or not of a natural origin hold more density. When we consume foods that have not been tampered with and come straight from the earth, they carry more life force energy, which fuels our own life force. This is what you might call whole foods or living foods. They are life-giving. When you eat packaged or highly modified foods, these carry a denser frequency and can weigh you down energetically and physically. Whatever we put into our temple that is dense creates disharmony within us. When we feed ourselves in light, we integrate more light and nourish our soul.

As beings in physical form, it can be a delicious experience to savor an exceptional meal, purchase a new outfit, or get our hands on the latest technology. Yet when there is an over-reliance on physical items or substances, it weighs us down. Eating for the pure joy and sustenance of this act is much different than eating to avoid feeling our emotions or only finding delight in food consumption and nowhere else. Buying a new pair of shoes because they are comfortable and express your unique style is quite different from buying new shoes compulsively because you're trying to fill a void from within.

Hoarding would be an extreme example of taking on density. Whenever we form an attachment to something, we anchor ourselves in density. Whether consciously or unconsciously, we can attach ourselves to people, circumstances, or things, and the attachment forms when we believe we *need* that thing or person. As we relinquish the ego's need and remember that everything we need is within us, we free ourselves of the density that otherwise binds us.

Density forms in your heart when you close your heart, when you find reasons to stop trusting life. Life is constantly generating an opportunity for you to see through the eyes of love, but when you stop trusting life, fear becomes the lens through which you perceive. When we are distrusting and in defense mode, we are closed off from ease, enjoyment, and authentic self-expression. Our energy is thickened, dense, and rigid. We move slowly, as if we're making our way through molasses.

Our dreams, needs, and desires feel like they take an eternity to manifest. While our mind may be running a thousand miles a minute, our desired creations come to fruition slowly. Our unconscious, self-sabotaging patterns, fears, and limitations hold us back from creating at God-speed, which is our true, divine pace. As you move through the murkiness of unconscious realities, patterns, emotions, and beliefs, you always have a choice to continue engaging with them at the same level of understanding they were created or shedding the light of your greater awareness on them. We shed this light by elevating to meet the consciousness of our Higher Self, our fuller expression.

To match our soul's perspective, we stop pretending that our limitations are the absolute truth, final, or all-encompassing. We honor what we have gone through and the part of us that has felt the pain and restriction from those perceived limitations, but we do not need to entertain them any longer. We are free to unpack the baggage and let our soul emerge. It is our sovereign right to free ourselves more and more.

Cleaning Your Inner Closet

As you gain conscious awareness of the places inside of you that are inauthentic and ego-driven, that awareness shifts your motivations and intentions. Eventually, your soul's intentions become your only intentions. When you are wise enough to let the old strategies, struggles, and survival mechanisms go, you gain more freedom in your process of co-creation. Imagine someone saying to you, "You know you can set those heavy burdens down, don't you?" Yet you fight for your hardships and your heartbreaks, saying that the world is filled with people who hurt you and circumstances that let you down, so you must hold on to these burdens because they will protect you from getting hurt again.

Little do you know that these burdens do not protect you—they hold you back from aligning to a reality where things are easier, smoother, and where people are loving and kind. When we are drenched in the heavy, sticky energies of separation consciousness, it can be difficult to feel or have this clarity, to be reunited with this universal law: As within, so without. It is in our highest interest to clean our inner closet, to bring awareness to the skeletons in there, to dust the blinds and let the light shine in.

Our Higher Self wants to shine forth, but it cannot be housed in this density; the heavy energies hold our soul back from fully emerging. Our Higher Self is actively working to help us move dense energies out, activate our light body, and open our heart so that we can become a vibrational match for soul embodiment to occur. We can do our part by tending to our temple: our physical body, our energy body, our emotional body, our mental body. We can bring conscious awareness to these parts that make up the whole. We bring that same awareness, that divine loving energy, that stream of well-being to those parts that were frozen in trauma, separation, and fear as they step forward in our present-moment experiences. As we focus lovingly on these parts, we melt the density and we're uplifted into those lighter frequencies.

Imagine you've invited a dear friend to come and stay with you. But you haven't cleaned your house for months—everything is strewn about, you haven't dusted or mopped, and the trash has been piling up for weeks. Your guest walks into the room where she's supposed to stay and there's litter everywhere. There's no room on the bed for her to lie down, and the place smells like garbage. She looks at you and wonders why you haven't prepared a clean space for her. She thinks, *I can't breathe in this room, it's so dusty and smelly*, and she has to leave. She wishes she could spend more time with you, but she needs a more comfortable sacred space where she feels respected and honored.

We respect our soul by clearing the density, by cleaning house. We make room for our soul to emerge, to match the vibration of our soul's expression, so that it may come through us and shine forth. In doing this, our Higher Self can then step forward and guide our life more and more, merge with us, and co-create the magic and miracles that we so wish for. When we disrespect our soul, shutting it out, saying, "I want it *my* way, I'm not going to surrender, I want control," we run in vicious circles. If only we'd be willing to work in collaboration *with* our soul, as our soul. When we are consciously focused on walking our soul's path, we are deliberately moving toward higher and higher consciousness, circumstances, and beauty.

DANIELLE KORT

Raising Your Vibrational Frequency

Energies are meant to move, transform, and evolve, just as you as a soul are meant to. When dense energy becomes stagnant in your physical vessel or within your field, it obstructs the flow of life force energy, which is meant to circulate through you. In Chinese medicine, meridians in the body act as highways to transport Chi, this same life-giving energy. When those meridians become blocked by toxins or dense thought and emotional debris, it can cause illness and disease. As we purify the dense energies of our physical apparatus, we clear the way for the light of our soul to flow freely through us.

Purging the density from our beingness naturally activates more light within us and raises our vibrational frequencies. We can initiate this process of activating and raising our light frequencies ourselves, and this also clears density from our system. We can do this by tuning ourselves to a higher vibrational frequency moment by moment. Much like tuning to a different, more preferred television channel, we can tune ourselves to channels that feel lighter and brighter, more peaceful and vibrant.

By tuning in to and immersing ourselves in activities that bring us joy and fulfillment, we move into resonant fields of consciousness, and our energy is transformed and uplifted. Here, it is easier to guide ourselves into more loving and optimistic thoughts and emotions as we are now in energetic resonance with them. In this space, we are able to receive light codes and universal information from the sun and this planetary being known as Gaia, as she too is ascending into her higher dimensional expression.

We can raise our vibrational frequency by focusing on and tuning to thoughts of appreciation and feelings of gratitude. We can focus on lighthearted humor and let go of the over-serious and fearful attitudes of the conditioned ego mind. We can pet our dogs and cats, play with our pets, come back to our innocence. We can go into nature, put our bare feet on the earth, and allow Mother Nature to help us realign and reharmonize.

We can rise in frequency by opening our hearts, stretching our bodies, doing breath work or sound healing. We can meditate, dance, or fully relax and unwind. You can feel it when you get that whole-y flow circulating through your field. It can be quite a palpable sensation once you become accustomed to sensing this energy. Like all things, practice leads to mastery, and this can be life-changing as you incorporate these practices into your everyday life.

Remember that energy is constantly moving, shifting, and transforming. Energy is never *truly* stagnant or stuck. With our pure intentions and choice to uplift our vibrational frequency, we can manifest so-called miracles. It is truly miraculous to move beyond the dense energetics of what you once thought made up the entirety of your world and into a state of being so profound, so pristine, that you hardly recognize your surroundings. And yet, this is what you as a soul are here to experience. We don't find our way home by continuing to bump around in the dark, unconscious corners of our minds. We must look up to the light, move toward it, and expand it from the core of our being.

Dissolving this density is truly a process. It's not a magic pill you take once, and, poof, you're free and at peace. It's a moment-by-moment choice to focus back on that center point of stillness where all is well, where you are safe, where you are free to express yourself joyfully, fully, boundlessly. It is a remembering. Those ancient rememberings simply get clouded, covered up, and overlaid with limiting beliefs, which stifle and suppress the expansive soul. They were only constructs that gave us a particular experience, and we signed up for that experience. Yet we are always being and becoming, shifting and transforming, birthing and being birthed. We are true adventurers at our core.

When we find our inner light, remembering that we are light, and begin to see ourselves and others in our highest light as our true essence, this expands our consciousness and lightens our load. Our frequency rises and we once again see through the eyes of immaculate love. Our realities shift to match our new vibration, and our world becomes colorful and bright. Rather than being weighed down by the old, unconscious programs, conditioning patterns, emotional baggage, and archaic paradigms, we grow wings and we are able to soar. We take flight as we learn to let go and surrender the heavy burdens entirely.

CHAPTER 3—BREATHING PEACE

Breath is life. When we disconnect from our breath because of things like trauma, fear, and shock, it obstructs our life force energy and our innate creative capacities. This resistance causes us to react to life rather than generate life. We then find ourselves repeatedly stopped by this perpetual fear that we continue to manifest as we engage with it. When you find yourself triggered by a certain person or situation, it is a normal coping mechanism to lose touch with your breath and react with a fight, flight, or freeze response.

When you don't meet these moments with conscious awareness and conscious breath, you experience ongoing resistance and limitation. Your dreams or desires are stunted again and again. This happens when we lose touch with the present moment and go back into the fears of our mind.

You can use your breath to reconnect with this eternal now. Your breath can help you soothe those parts of you that had become frozen in trauma and fearful perspectives. Breath is the portal to your fullest expression. It is an integrative catalyst.

Holding your breath out of fear fragments you from your wholeness and holds you back from this fullness. It causes you to shut yourself down, and if you don't address these automatic reactions born of fear, you move toward an experience of death. It is important to give your body plenty of oxygen to maintain and sustain your experience of life. Experiences in a world of separation consciousness have caused you to feel unsafe, but it is now your soul's purpose to move you back into a safe environment from within.

Soothing the Inner Child: Healing Emotional Trauma

As young children, we feel freer to express ourselves candidly and openly. Yet there come moments along our journey that threaten our sense of safety, and this ability to live in peace and express with joyful exuberance becomes constricted. In these moments, if a parent, for instance, acts from a place of fear and cries "no" with a panicked, fearful tone, this can cause a child to react in that same fear-based frequency. In this moment, you, as a child, are unable to process what is actually happening. You go into the fear frequency and go unconscious. You abandon the present moment. You don't mean to, but this fear overtakes you and gets stored in your energetic field and physical body.

Let's say this parent or caretaker screamed "NO!!" when they saw you were about to run into the street, and so while they were well-meaning and had your highest level of safety in mind, they inadvertently introduced this fearful reaction into your reality. The shock of this fear disallows you from understanding what has truly taken place, and so you create your own story about this event. You come to believe that you've done something very bad and you avoid making mistakes at all costs going forward. When life hands you a golden opportunity, you avoid taking the leap for fear of any risk of "messing up" that might be associated. This imprint drives your choices into adulthood and in some instances, for numbers of lifetimes.

Now, even if a parent were to unleash all of their inner pain and turmoil onto you, it's never their true intention from the level of soul. They simply don't have the tools or awareness to show up in unconditional love, as in this case, all they know is how to project their pain onto another. So rather than placing blame on those who you feel hurt you or introduced fearful perspectives or energy into your world, you can begin to open your heart to the realization that all beings you encounter along your life's journey have also experienced these moments that took *their* breath away and caused them to sink into fear. We can reclaim our power by simply taking responsibility for our own energy system and letting the details of the story we created surrounding those fearful moments go. Then we are able to deal exclusively with the aftermath or the residual energetics.

We can see these moments when we go unconscious and sink back into fearful perspectives as traumatic in nature, and these traumas get stored inside us. We are constantly creating our individual realities through our consciousness, through what we hold in our energetic field, and through the physical actions we take. So, if there was a fear or trauma that you were unable to process as a child or even in a past life experience, this remains in your field of consciousness.

It might be twenty years after you had this traumatic childhood experience described above, and let's say you're at work typing away on your computer. You see your manager approaching and she doesn't look happy. She stops at your desk and alerts you that you've made a mistake. There's fear in her tone of voice because this mistake might cost the company a lot of money. This fearful reaction brings you right back to that moment as a child when you had exchanged within this fearful interaction. You lose touch with your breath, your hands get clammy, and you're unable to respond to your manager in an articulate or clear manner. In fact, you can't respond at all. You've returned to the original trauma, and it's as if you are four years old again. In essence, you *are* four years old in this moment, as your inner toddler has stepped forward so that her fear-based perspective can be reframed.

In moments like this, being especially kind and gentle with ourselves is paramount for our healing. These triggering situations are opportunities to usher these frightened parts of us back into safety with our unconditional love so that eventually, we can remain present in all moments, in all situations. When you are in the midst of a triggering exchange, it can be supportive to step away from the situation so you can regain your centeredness and sense of safety before you go back in to respond. If you find yourself in the kind of situation described above, know that you could simply excuse yourself to go to the restroom or take a break. Use this moment of stepping away to return to your breath and the present moment. If you can't easily excuse yourself, or the exchange took place and you find yourself in the aftermath (whether that be hours, days, or even years later), you can still reflect on what happened and do the inner child work (described below) at this later time.

In a quiet space, return to presence by slowing your breath, opening your heart and soothing yourself back to safety. Then, from your adult or higher self perspective, connect with your inner child aspect who has been triggered. Give yourself a big hug, imagining your inner child is in your arms. Allow any emotions that want to surface to be acknowledged and felt fully, knowing that as they express, they will move through and out of you. We can be a space of compassionate grace while simultaneously feeling our inner child's heavier emotions.

Ask your inner child what they need in this moment. You will often find that what they need is love. So give this to them, right here and right now. Speak to your inner child like you would any child, with patience and compassion, letting them know that their viewpoint or reaction to the situation is valid (not shameful or unacceptable). Help your inner child to see that you are here to love and protect them and that they are not alone as you gently guide them back to inner peace and safety from within.

Now that you have regulated your nervous system, expand the inner light from your higher heart and shine it on the situation at hand. Extend this compassionate light to all parties involved, including yourself. Now, you can reframe the story or belief that causes you to manifest these triggering experiences. In the example described above, you can ask yourself what you have learned from this experience. Perhaps you come to realize that what is needed is greater compassion for yourself.

You can reframe your fear of making mistakes and consequently getting in trouble, to understanding from a higher perspective, that you are continually learning and evolving and that acting unconsciously is simply an opportunity for you to grow your awareness and refine your creational process. Perhaps, now you can see how having compassion for yourself, even when the other person doesn't have patience or practice with this, actually sets a positive example for them to learn from as well.

From here, you can go back to your manager, or whoever who has triggered you (if it applies) to see how this situation might be rectified. By returning to the conversation as a more grounded and centered version of yourself, rather than from your triggered old identity, you open up a greater possibility for mutually beneficial solutions to emerge.

In doing this inner work to unconditionally love each of your inner aspects that became stuck in trauma or frozen in fear, you raise your consciousness, you lighten your load, and gradually, all fear will melt away. You become better and better at remaining present and staying conscious in those moments that trigger those fearful, stuck places inside of you. Learning to come from divine love and compassion more and more eases the process and uplifts your vibration so that you see fewer of these triggering reflections.

You Are beyond Safe

Safety is your natural state of being. It is at the core of all that you truly are. If you look around the room you're in, or the elements if you're reading this out in nature, in this present moment, you can see that all is well. Nothing exists outside of... This ... Right ... Here. Look at your hands, the grass beneath you, or the wall before you, and feel the presence of *this very moment*. Feel the wellspring of well-being within you.

The roots of conscious awareness are the deepest, most profound sense of safety you can imagine, even beyond that. It is only in moments of unconsciousness that you venture off from what you know to be true within. These moments of unsafety that take your breath away cause emotional and mental resistance that materialize as disharmonic imprints within your body and energetic field. We can soothe these spaces and places by sitting in quietude and reflection, allowing this resistance to surface and be retuned, reshaped, and reintegrated back into the unified field.

If this resistance manifests as a physical experience, we simply meet it with conscious awareness and love it back into the present moment. Eventually, all resistance created from a sense of unsafety will be reunited with peace. Disharmony or dis-ease only comes when we are seeing through the lens of separation consciousness and fear-based perspectives, when we are battling with different aspects of us or those in our outer world reflections. Love is the integrative agent that binds and soothes all that is fragmented or out of tune.

Learn to be gentle with yourself in this unification process, tending to yourself like an innocent young child. In doing this, you will find much greater ease in retuning yourself back to the divine frequency of love. If a young child were struggling to learn how to walk, for instance, you wouldn't scream at the child, "Get it together! Figure it out already!" You would exercise patience and compassion and continue to share all that you know in order to support this young child's process. You would know that screaming wouldn't be supportive to their growth and may actually cause considerable damage on their evolutionary path, as perpetuating unsafety causes resistance or fragmentation in the child's being. When we can treat those aspects of ourselves with that same tender love and care, shepherding them back to safety, we accelerate our progress in harmonizing our inner and outer worlds.

When a child feels safe within herself, she feels free to express herself in creative and loving ways. She easily exudes joy and passion in what she creates and how she expresses. Her imagination is open and untamed, and she goes on to bless others with her magnificent presence. As each human learns to come back to this place inside of them, it co-creates a world of peace, love, and harmony. This is not a pipe dream; it is the dream of your Spirit, the collective dream of unity.

Relaxing the Mind

Learning how to return to peace is a practice of quieting your busy mind. When you find your mind wandering off onto tangents, simply bring yourself back to the present moment by touching your hand and feeling into your body. When you are solely focused in a mind-based perspective, you're separating from the full potential of your conscious awareness.

You are not simply your mind, although this is a powerful tool when you know how to use it. Before you can access your divine or universal mind, which is in resonance with your soul's perspective, you must first learn to quiet the small, linear mind, which is separated by ego identities and their programmed thoughts, fears, and limitations. This is why it is so impactful to take time and space away from your busy routine and sit with yourself in stillness. Even ten minutes a day in a meditative practice can be enough to reset your nervous and neurological systems.

Standing in line or driving a car can be great opportunities to practice meditation, as ultimately, you're relaxing your need to follow streams of thought and instead you're focusing solely here with present moment awareness. If you can come to a place where you realize there's nowhere else you'd rather be than here in this beautiful present moment, you are already freeing yourself from the pulls and tugs of a restless, separated mind. Peace comes naturally when you aren't regretting, worrying, or wishing you were somewhere else.

Use your breath to return to this now moment. It is in this moment that all things can be made new. As we return to presence and alignment with our Source, that which was separated from Divinity inside of us can return to wholeness. A tumor heals spontaneously or a flatlined heartbeat is restored. What we consider a miracle is really just a return to our loving, harmonious, most natural state of well-being.

Feel into where you may be holding tension in your body or your energetic field. Breathe space into that area, feeling the old density dissolving as you bring in a flow of new light quotients. Allow this light to burn away the density, the heaviness, the aches or pains. Know that it is possible for these densities to be transformed in an instant. Again, a miracle is really just a shift in perception, a deep faith in Source/God/the Universe, a relaxing into this "all is well" energy, which is constantly flowing through us.

Trust in this flow of energy, allowing it to circulate throughout your entire being, cleansing your physical body, etheric body, mental body, and emotional bodies. Use your breath to open the dams and bring forth the light. Trust in yourself and love yourself enough to let the light in. Those universal purified energies exist within our core, not "out there" somewhere far away. They exist in the seed of our consciousness.

On the in-breath, open your heart, and on the out-breath, let go of the dense energies, feeling them fall away. Unity Consciousness is pulling you *in*. You are the only one resisting that reunion. Your natural state wants to be expressed, wants to be remembered. Allow this energy to pull you in and expand you out, enveloping you in this pure, unconditional love. Let it relax you and transform you, melting those frozen, fearful states.

When you allow yourself to fully relax, beyond thought, beyond control, you come to find yourself melting into a kind of orgasmic bliss, as if you're being cradled by the cosmos, held by the Divine Mother and Father. Not a care in the world could draw your attention away. You are wrapped in a soft, warm blanket of unwavering peace, and you cannot wipe the smile from your face as your heart is beaming with joyful exuberance. Here, all is well, and you are as light as a feather.

Becoming Aware of Your Creative Thoughts

We are these energetic and physical beings simultaneously, which are actually one and the same, as the physical is also energy and has only materialized through our energetic focus and creative thought. So that means even our bodies are a manifestation. We manifest our physical appearance and physical states through our thoughts, through our emotional body, and onto paper, so to speak, onto the canvas of our life, onto the physical plane.

Picture a young professional who has been stressed out, living under high pressure, working a demanding job, and you'll see the evidence of that relentless stress appearing in their physical manifestation: wrinkles on their forehead, prematurely graying hair, maybe some excess weight has been gained, through those actions the person takes or is not taking when they live in a world of stress - *their own world in the making.*

You create your universe according to your picture of reality, and this picture is framed by your beliefs. Your beliefs are just the thoughts you think repeatedly and are often automatic or subconscious. But they're only subconscious because you haven't brought your conscious awareness to them yet. As you expand your conscious awareness, all of those thoughts and beliefs that were once subconscious or unconscious now become conscious.

You do this by returning to this present moment, to your heart, to safety, where you can see clearly; by returning to the divine frequency of love, where you can perceive coherently. You don't have access to shifting unconscious beliefs when you're acting in unconscious ways or by thinking and feeling without conscious awareness. These unconscious ways are born of fear and separation and all the emotional turmoil that comes with that. When your vibration is dense, it's because you are latching onto these limiting beliefs and ways of doing things. You're running around in survival mode trying to make ends meet, too concerned with meeting your ego's expectations and feeding your belief in lack and scarcity. This keeps you dumbed down, dulled down, weighed down.

Changing the Channel: From Surviving to Thriving

Let's say you're in a rush because you're late for a meeting. You're fumbling around in your purse, trying to find your keys. You don't remember where you put them, but you know they must be in there because you always put them in your purse. This frantic energy causes you to knock your purse onto the ground and everything goes flying out. You're shaking in panic because this meeting could mean big things for your career. You can't believe this is happening today of all days. You crumple to the floor in tears. You cry and cry and cry until there are no more tears left. After a few minutes, you take a breath and notice that everything is really quiet. You don't even hear any thoughts in your head. You have the sense that all is well, even though your mind might like to think otherwise. Then you receive an intuitive nudge to check that small zippered back pocket of your purse. You can't believe it, but the keys were there all along.

These moments of rushing around are because your ego identity has you believing that these are life-or-death situations, and this has you fighting for your survival. It is in these moments that you lose touch with your inner knowing and you don't have access to things like your memory or even simple answers to questions another may ask you. It is in slowing down and bringing yourself back to presence that all the answers you will ever need can come forward and present themselves.

Fear is just a dense vibrational sequence. When you feel fear and act upon it, you are tuning in to a network of limited and distorted perception. Much like a radio dial, you can tune your frequency to different channels. For a time, the human collective has tuned in to and agreed upon denser frequencies or channels based in fear. Yet as an individual expression, you have the free will to change your channel.

Unless you continue to look around and say, "I guess this is all that's available to me," you have the freedom to explore other options. Until you begin retuning your vibrational frequency, much of what you see "out there" is lack, limitation, and survival-based matrixes playing out in the physical world. These structures that have been created, which keep you running on a hamster wheel chasing after things you believe you must acquire or accomplish, have been put in place by survival-based thinking. You have learned to use your logical mind to map out how you will make your life work. Rather than working with your energy and your innate inner knowing, you burden yourself with the heavy lifting of something that you could easily outsource to your true Source: Your Spirit, Higher Self, God.

When you exist in a world of separation, you believe you must go it alone, figure it all out yourself, and then strive to make it all happen. This creates a lot of unnecessary stress, strife, and struggle. It's not wrong, but there are easier, more enjoyable ways to create. When you believe in lack, you grind away and compete to secure your little slice of some finite pie in the sky. If you are not constantly doing or achieving, you believe your resources will run out and you will be left to fend for yourself on the streets. This fear drives you as you frantically thrash through the murky waters of survival consciousness.

From the human perspective we often think of survival as something you must fight for, compete for, and win based upon the genes you inherited, the level of schooling you've completed, or your proficiencies in business. Even if you're ignoring your true wants and desires, you think, *At least I'll be able to put a roof over my head or a meal on my table for another day.* At this level of understanding, there is never enough. You take the scraps when deep down, you know you're worthy of more. From a soul perspective, survival is not about physical acquisitions as much as it is about the energetics of your consciousness. If you are only existing just to get by, you are giving your body the message that there's not enough to go around and that you need to operate on a short supply of energy.

Here is where you restrict the flow of life force energy and your creative capacities are squashed. When you expand beyond this limited perception, knowing that you are always supported when you choose life-affirming thoughts, feelings, and actions, you begin to exist in a new world altogether. Life supports your survival when you *choose* life. There is an ever-abundant supply of all that you ever truly need when you relax into the truth of what you are and what you are one with, and when you establish a deep trust in life.

From an energetic perspective, when you cling to a belief in scarcity, you dim your light. Yet this light is the true fuel that keeps you going, keeps you flowing, keeps you alive. So trusting in your Spirit, your Inner light, to guide your way, rather than gripping in fear to scarcity thinking, is what *actually* ensures your survival. But not only that, it aligns you to a world where you are thriving, where you are truly joyful and passionate about life.

Survival consciousness is but a fearful conception of the mind. When you can relax and trust in the flow of your life's unfolding, the idea of survival becomes inapplicable, and thriving becomes your new way of life. As you follow the whispers from within, your soul's guidance, you will find your hand naturally reaching to receive the ripe apple, which has just fallen from the tree beside you. You will find yourself slowly putting it up to your lips and enjoying its sweet nectar, feeling the appreciation for this graceful gift from the earth.

You will find yourself naturally picking up the phone to call someone you love who's been on your mind. You will see someone in a tough spot, and without much effort at all, you will share with them the wisdom you have gleaned along your own life's journey, which helped you move through that same circumstance.

When you cease the need to continually ask, What's in it for me? What will I get out of this? and instead ask, How might I use my God-given gifts to serve the greater good of all? you flip the energetics from survival, from grasping and striving, to thriving. This is because what you put out is what you get back. So, when you make it a priority to share with others, to support others, you are also sharing this bounty with yourself.

The "little me" tries to gather all it can, like a squirrel gathering its nuts to survive through the winter. But the soul is seasonless and knows that all the nuts it will ever need will present themselves in divine right timing as it treads its path of serving the greater good of all. You do not need millions in the bank to feel safe or secure. When you trust your Higher Self and your life's journey, you can feel safe and secure in every moment regardless of your circumstances, what's in the bank, or what's happening around you.

Home in Your Higher Heart

Opening your heart is a gift you give to yourself and others. Nature naturally helps you do this as it aligns you back to your true essence, where you are always safe, where you *know* you are safe, and where you trust life with every ounce of your being. We only find it challenging to open our heart and keep it open when we hold on to things like resentment, unforgiveness, and bitterness; when we find "evidence" and say, "See? This happened, so I can no longer trust myself, others, or the world around me."

Your defensive ego identities try to protect you and your heart from possible future hurts. Here, we build heart walls and then sometimes stone-cold castles around our heart, complete with a moat around the castle, which seemingly guards us against getting hurt. When we work to create defense strategies to protect ourselves from danger, what we've actually done is close our heart. This hinders your ability to connect with others in deep and meaningful ways. Yet it is only when you form attachments or energetic cords to others and view things personally through the lens of persona that you perceive any given interaction as hurtful or painful. It is only in seeing others as separate from yourself that you hang the Closed for Business sign on your heart.

Our heart relates us in an emotional way to those around us, helping us connect to our humanity. Have you ever listened to a love song that reminded you of your ex-lover or romantic partner and then you yearned for their love? Just one more kiss or hug from this person who had touched your heart would be so sweet. This song reminds you of their scent, their smile, or that beautiful night you danced under the stars barefoot on your back patio. This is the experience of being human and of being in relationship with others while connecting from your heart. It is a purposeful part of your evolutionary journey as a light being in human form.

It is our higher heart that holds the keys and codes to a more expanded and universal experience of love. As we evolve our consciousness, our heart expands and merges with our higher heart, where we perceive through the lens of a more unified perspective. Let's say in one instance that you take someone's comment very personally, and you harbor a resentment inside your heart. In another instance, while connecting from your higher heart, you can clearly see that this person's comment has to do with the pain they hold inside of themselves and really has nothing to do with you. Here, you have compassion for this person and may even be able to support them in finding love for themselves rather than projecting their pain onto others.

Our higher heart has an intelligence of its own. We can ask our higher heart to support us in seeing our life's situations from a higher perspective so that we have a deeper level of compassion for all beings. From this vantage point, we can see that love is not only meant to be shared with our romantic partner, our children, our family, but equally with all life forms. We realize that love is our true nature and that conditional love is not true love.

Anything less than the divine frequency of love is simply a disharmonic frequency that can be retuned or simply surrendered to Source. Life is constantly asking you if you are ready to return to love, if you are ready to let go of everything you have burdened yourself with that conflicts with your true, loving nature. How would you answer this question? How might you show up in love regardless of what has happened before? Seeing through the eyes of love, acting from love, is a moment-by-moment choice until it becomes our natural embodied expression once again.

We can see love as this ever-present current of energy that fuels us, and it is only in venturing away from our truth, which is based in love, which *is* love, that we slow this flow of energy. Some call this flow of energy prana, Chi, Qi, kundalini, or life force energy. In essence, it is all one. We can allow love to fuel our interactions, our creations, or we can shut it out and try to find energy from exterior sources like caffeine or ego-driven motivations. One will fuel us eternally and the other will cause us to crash and burn again and again.

DANIELLE KORT

The Peace in Wholeness

The universal stream of well-being surges through your body, through your field, more powerfully as you merge and integrate each of your soul aspects into Unity Consciousness. When these parts or versions of us surface, we meet them with our love and patience, with our compassion. You may feel engulfed in the heaviness as they emerge, but know that they are surfacing so they can be set free. We visit and return to these heavy emotional spaces and places so that we can clean them up and lighten the burdens we've been carrying around. Rather than allowing these intense emotions to sink you back into these painful perspectives, what you are tasked with doing is to uplift them with the light of your soul. In doing this, you *lighten* your load. You become enlightened.

As they emerge in our awareness, we can soothe those parts of us that got stuck in fear, or seemingly stuck, but that are actually just replaying or re-engaging with old, fearful stories. These old, fearful stories are like watching a horror movie: You can't take your eyes off of it; you're glued to the screen. You want to look away but you can't—at least you don't *think* you can. You're so involved in the plot; it feels so real. And yet ... it's just a movie. You have permission to put down the popcorn, be with those frightened parts of you, love them, and help them melt away the fear.

Breathing peace is what is natural for you. Breathing this tranquility, this frequency of divine love, which is available to you in every moment, harmonizes your being and opens your heart on its own accord. These high vibrational energetic frequencies are like notes or chords in a song, and your soul's song is made up of these frequencies. You breathe, live, and play them through your presence and dedication to living in present awareness. You tune into presence with your pure intention and by your choice to surrender.

So surrender the cares, worries, and burdens of your outer world happenings and focus back into this loving place of presence. This is what aligns every part of you back to wholeness, back to your natural state of well-being. The more you surrender to your Spirit, your higher, innate inner knowing, the more you unify from within and the higher your vibration rises. Your soul vibrates in these higher states of consciousness, and as you rise to meet your soul's perspective, you gradually awaken from the fearful states that had once dominated your world. Peace is here for you, always and forever, and it would like to reunite you with its loving and gentle care. It is time for you to breathe peace in every living moment and for every *peace* of you to relax into its ease-filled and nurturing caress.

CHAPTER 4—WHISPERS FROM WITHIN

We each have an internal compass that guides us to make our highest, most soul-aligned choices, and eventually this leads us to embody all that we truly are. This inner compass is your true identity, your Higher Self or future self — the one who can see the larger picture and is readily available anytime you call upon it. Your Higher Self is continually trying to communicate with you and the more you tune in to these messages, which you might sense as whispers within you, among a number of other extra sensory signals, the more you become accustomed to discovering and decoding these messages.

So often, however, we learn to wear masks to hide our true identity for fear that others won't accept or love us. Have you ever stopped yourself from admitting your true feelings for fear of upsetting another person? Or perhaps you've led with your good looks, intelligence or humor because you're confident in that area, but secretly crave to be seen in a more wholistic way. What happens is that we have experiences, often originating in childhood or past lives, that cause us to believe our true identity must be hidden or filtered.

Let's imagine that you used your extra sensory perception in a past life with the intention of helping another see energetic blockages that prevented them from living their most joyous existence. But this other person couldn't understand your abilities and so they told the townspeople and you were called a witch and burned at the stake. How this might show up for you in this current life may be a fear of using your gifts and abilities. To play it safe you might ignore the fact that you can see beyond this physical reality and you keep this gift hidden behind a mask so that you don't pose as a threat to others, and in turn threaten your own safety. This mask becomes a persona which constantly tries to protect you from other potential future threats.

These ego identities or personas do not embody or represent the truth of our soul. These voices say things like, "Try to fit in or you'll be kicked out of the group." "You're not good enough as you are." "I'm unworthy of greater love." These voices tell us that we need to make a good impression so others will like us. We configure ourselves into pretzels, bending to meet the needs of these falsified voices, which we've unconsciously created.

We agree to do things we don't really want to do or feel called to do. We say, "Deep down, I knew that wasn't what was best for me, but I did it anyway." "Deep down" is our truth, our soul, the higher wisdom that gets buried underneath these ego identities we masquerade in to protect ourselves from a world of separation and fear. When we go out into our world and constantly react to the pain points of these personas, we become too busy, too distracted to hear that deep wisdom within.

It is in taking time out to reflect upon what is actually true for us versus what we have created from a painful perspective that we can begin to unravel the identities we had defined ourselves as. When considering a choice, you can ask yourself, Is this my highest choice in this now moment? The persona will point to past experiences as evidence for why you should choose from a place of fear, lack, and limitation. Perhaps in a rushed or dramatized manner, it will jump to protect you from the world of pain and suffering. Yet the whisper within you is strong and steady, calm and patient. When you first begin to listen to this inner calling, it may sound distant or quiet, but as you clear the dense programming of your ego identities, that inner voice, that inner knowing, grows louder and stronger.

As the human ego identity is formed, it is entrained and impressed upon by belief systems and emotional reactions born of lower dimensional frequencies. Our ego is not the problem, but when the ego is turned against itself and others through societal programming, it causes disharmony and destruction, both internally and in our outer world. So when you come from this perspective, things can feel foggy, groggy, and unclear. Your mind races, you feel lost and confused, and your heart feels heavy and broken. You are never truly lost, though, because in any moment, you can reconnect with that larger part of you, the true you, which is eternally at home and at peace within. It becomes a choice then to either continue running through an endless maze of unconscious programming and conditioning or open your eyes, zoom out and see the maze for what it truly is: an entanglement of your energy with things that are not in alignment with what and who you truly are.

These entanglements anchor you to lower dimensional experiences, but they are things that can be renounced and surrendered to your Spirit. At one time, you grasped onto these limiting belief systems, these realities based in fear. This is because you didn't know that anything else existed outside of them and because your ego identity seeks to find safety within these separate, definitive structures. You may have looked around and noticed everyone else operating in these ways, and so perhaps you thought to yourself, *Well, this is just the way it is!*

Yet at some point, you grew weary of these superficial and restrictive ways. And then you thought to yourself, *There must be more!* And so here you are, looking to disentangle yourself from this maze of the limited mind, this "rat race" that has you perceiving through painful perspectives. These perspectives are only painful because they are not in harmony with your true essence. They simply served you for a temporary experience, and you are here to expand beyond that now.

When you give yourself time and space to get quiet and tune in to the whispers from within, you are giving yourself the gift of clarity and guidance. Yet it is not only listening to this inner voice that will bring about great transformation. It is essential that you take heed and follow that guidance, taking that inspired action, which comes to you in those instances of present-moment awareness. Whether you're meditating, walking in nature, or taking a shower when the inspiration hits, following up with those action steps causes you to shift to higher, lighter, and brighter realities. It's common to hear the inner guidance and then immediately judge it with your logical mind, saying things like, *That doesn't make sense. Why would I do that?* Yet the key is to trust and follow this guidance with your faithful heart, knowing that it is a breadcrumb on a trail leading you to wonderful lands yet unknown.

Our inner guidance comes in many forms, whether it be a voice from within, pictures in your third eye or imagination, a feeling sensation like goosebumps, or simply knowing something without understanding how you know. When you tune in to this guidance, you might feel light or expansive, you might feel a sense of excitement or passion, and this feeling is what lets you know that it's aligned with your soul's perspective. The linear mind may try to rationalize and give reasons why this guidance won't work or might put you at risk, yet this feeling is to confirm what you already know deep down.

Start by asking your Higher Self to show you what a yes feels like and what a no feels like. With a yes, your body/energy body may feel open, expansive, light, warm, tingly, joyful. With a no, your body may feel any of the following sensations: closed off, contracted, icky, heavy, dense, sluggish. You can then ask your Higher Self or inner guidance if a certain choice is in your highest and best interest by simply getting quiet, focusing on your breath, and asking the question silently or aloud. *Is this choice in my highest and best interest?* Then wait for the yes or no response.

With this messaging system in place, you can ask your Higher Self limitless questions about your life choices and directions. Your inner guidance shows you whether that choice or path will lead to higher, lighter, brighter, more expansive experiences or ones that are more limiting or difficult. As you learn to flow with your inner guidance, you automatically dissolve densities within you because you move beyond them, expanding into lighter realities based in love.

Living in Alignment

When we perceive through the lens of our soul or Higher Self, we are in alignment. Alignment is our birthright. It is our greater truth. Living or perceiving outside of this alignment causes us to feel heavy, confused, and unresolved. We distrust life, and we look outside ourselves for answers or solutions to help us feel better.

When we can recognize that misalignment is simply a disharmonic frequency, something that we can retune from within, we become empowered to reunite with our alignment again and again. Alignment is not something generally taught in school or by your caretakers, but it is something very innate, very natural to you. You know you are in alignment when there is peace inside your heart, when you are living and playing in joy, and when your soul speaks to you and you listen by taking the inspired action steps given.

When you're in alignment, your thoughts, emotions, beliefs, and actions are in sync. Your intentions, on all levels, are in congruence. Disharmony, or a pulling away from your soul perspective, causes resistance inside of you and in the reflections of your life or dream. The vibrational frequency of this misalignment feels fatiguing and burdensome. When you don't feel good in your body, in your mind or emotions, you know there is a misalignment at play.

If you've ever received chiropractic work, you know that an adjustment brings your spine and surrounding bones and joints back into alignment so your body can return to harmony and well-being. Similarly, when you bring each of your bodies of consciousness back into harmonization and collaboration, you return to vibrational alignment. This vibrational coherence eventually manifests in your physicality as well. If you experience conflict inside yourself, where different parts of you want different things or are working against each other, you may experience dis-ease in your physical expression. Yet when all the parts of you work in unison, you will experience harmony, ease, and well-being in your physicality, in your health. Returning to your soul's perspective, or your highest vibrational alignment, is what unifies each of your fragmented aspects and bodies of consciousness.

When you aren't living in alignment with your soul, when you're not being true to yourself, it takes extra energy to negotiate with those parts of you that are resisting your truth. That push and pull, that wishy-washy energy, takes up mental and emotional space within you. It makes it more difficult to direct your will, your energy, toward that which your soul truly wants. You might make a choice that feels easier in the moment but is actually more challenging in the long run. These choices that don't honor your soul, but continue the old, habitual cycles of resistance, create more turmoil within you. This turmoil shows up as confusion, thoughts running in all directions, emotional rollercoasters, and clutter within your field, which can turn into dis-ease within your physical body. So every choice you make that *does* align with your soul's truth merges your energy more and more back into unity, back into the unified field.

When you clean up those disharmonic frequencies, it becomes easier to hear the whispers from within, the callings of your soul. There's greater clarity here, more space for awareness to pierce through, more space for presence. Your soul is able to step forward more easily and guide your path more powerfully when you get out of your own way. When you clear the clutter, you find stillness inside.

It takes practice to hear your soul's clarity, distinguishing it from the trappings of your conditioned mind. You get better and better at distinguishing it by listening for what is innate within you and by taking that inspired action moment by moment. When we are so focused on what is happening in our outer world, with our to-do lists, dramas, and distractions, we lose touch with what wants to be communicated from inside of us, from present moment awareness.

The Gift of Presence

Presence is a present, a gift. For most people, experiencing this gift is a rarity, as they are constantly doing, chasing, or seeking things outside of themselves. Tuning in to presence is less of an action and more of a surrender. We have been conditioned into "human *doings*," and yet we have come here to live an experience as human *beings*. To truly *be* with ourselves and others inside the gift of presence, we need to let go of the assessments, judgments, and assumptions we might otherwise make (about this moment, another person, or ourselves, for instance). In practicing presence, we can see ourselves and others as the divine beings we truly are. We are able to hold a space of deep love, compassion, honor, and respect for those before us, as well as for ourselves. Incredible beauty can unfold as you embody the gift of presence.

Practicing presence can come in many forms. Whether you sit quietly or lie down and continually bring your focus to this present moment, allowing the thoughts to float by or fall away rather than running off with them, or whether you bring your full focus to some simple activity, such as washing the dishes or driving a car, it's really about being fully here in this moment, which is all that truly exists. It's when we cling to the past and make the stories we created from those past experiences part of our identity, defining ourselves by these stories, that we cut ourselves off from presence. We limit others (in our mind) this way as well. What if you could see that your past does not define you? What if it were simply part of your experience and that experience does not need to determine what is within you or taking shape before you now?

It is a freeing realization to know that all things can be made new; that this moment is as fresh and limitless as we allow it to be. Our ego identity and the stories it has created boxes itself into definitive structures. It limits its capacities. Yet the formless Spirit within you is free of these restrictions and knows that all things are possible. It is only in this present moment that we have access to such limitless possibility.

Returning to this present moment, again and again, allows us to bring awareness to those places inside where we have limited ourselves. This awareness shines a light on those painful and limiting perspectives. We do not meet them with judgment or resentment but with loving kindness, knowing that they served a purpose for a certain amount of time. These structures and stories were put into place so that we could survive in a fearful world. Yet you have come to a place on your journey where you can see this fear-based world for what it is: a temporal illusory experience, a co-creative nightmare, if you will.

The way to dream a new dream is to steer your focus toward those things that light you up, impassion you, open your heart, and allow you to sing your song. In this new collective dream, your soul emerges to express openly, freely, and joyfully. Eventually, your soul, or Higher Self, is the only voice you hear. This happens as you discontinue allowing the fearful voices created by your ego to run the show. When we stop paying attention to and following these fearful voices, they become fainter and more distant and ultimately dissolve.

When making a choice, you can ask yourself, Does this truly nourish me? Does this serve the greatest good of all? The ego identity voices will care more about things like looking good in the eyes of others, gaining attention or approval, or trying to protect you from potential dangers, even if it means putting your well-being on the back burner. Your Higher Self, however, prioritizes your well-being and the well-being of all, in every moment. It knows that what's best for you is in alignment with what's best for all, as one's health cannot make another sicker, nor can one's wealth make another poorer. Yet your highest and best *can* uplift and inspire.

We can require a physical experience to show us which identities, densities, and limitations are ready to be retired, or we can sit in the sanctuary within, with our soul, as our soul, and allow what needs to be addressed, purified and cleared, be done from within. In doing this, discordant thoughts or emotions have space to bubble up, be acknowledged and expressed, and then let go. We may or may not have the back stories of where these thoughts or emotions came from, but we can know that true healing is occurring with greater ease and less pain and suffering, as often those physical experiences can be the two-by-fours that are hard lessons learned.

The difficulty in sitting with ourselves in pure presence often comes when we become afraid of *feeling*—feeling emotions that we perceive as overwhelming or painful. We can become afraid of facing those feelings, unsure if we'll be able to move through them. We might worry that we'll get stuck inside of our emotions if they surface, but this cannot happen. We may experience strong emotions longer than necessary, but only if we identify vehemently with them and hold on to them tightly. If we simply face our emotions, acknowledge them, and let them go, we allow true healing or vibrational attunement to occur.

You don't have to go this alone. You were never actually separate from the support, the love, and the guidance, as it has always been within you. There is much that can be done on your behalf when it comes to healing and harmonizing your frequencies and unifying your bodies of consciousness. Begin by relaxing your body and surrendering the cares or worries of your mind. Bring your awareness or focal point to your heart center and rest in the divine frequency of love. Here is where you can feel the presence of your spirit guides, whose assignment is to assist in your awakening process. When your sincere intention to heal, unify, and harmonize is coupled with your willingness to receive their assistance, your guides can support you in making the adjustments necessary for your greatest growth and expansion.

To receive this assistance, continually return to presence. The more we come back and drink from this wellspring of well-being, the more we align ourselves back to our truth, and that truth takes center stage in our lives once again. When you become grounded in yourself, rooted in presence, then the fears, resistance, or density simply fall away. The false premises become inapplicable, and your Spirit begins to soar, guiding you toward greater and greater awareness.

Practice listening for the whispers from within, from deep inside your core, and feel in your body, your energetic field, what this feels like. Feel the resonance of your soul and your soul's guidance. Understand what your sacred yes feels like from inside of you. Sense what your sacred no vibrates like. Ask what your most aligned choice is as you feel into where you're being guided from the depths of your higher heart. Rather than rushing ahead, pushing or forcing, fighting against, stalling, or resisting from your ego aspects ... be still. Sit in awareness and wait for the whispers from within. Wait for your heartstrings to play a beautiful song. Wait for the joy inside of you to bubble up and demonstrate that orgasmic "Yes!"

If it's not a full "yes," you will feel it. You will also feel those places inside that want you to lie to yourself to supposedly make it easier, to take a shortcut, to people please, to avoid what you know deep down. You do not need to entertain this. Withhold your own sacred boundary of "no" to those parts of you that want to ignore the whisper, want to ignore your deepest truth. The more you listen, the more you honor your soul, the stronger you become as you walk your path of sacred sovereignty.

Trusting Your Self

We often grow up learning to distrust ourselves because we assign greater significance to what our parents advise us to do, what our best friend thinks, what our teachers tell us, or the messages in the mass media. We draw conclusions based on what we're told *outside* of us. Your parents teach you things like learning how to walk, and this serves you. Then there are beliefs, opinions, and ways we learn to see the world that don't serve us, at least not anymore. These can be ancestral patterns, societal expectations, or ways of living that repress our soul's truth.

Our Higher Self/Future Self/Soul is constantly guiding us with a multitude of ways to get our attention, but when our attention is solely directed toward the old, outer world ways or the limiting lenses we have learned to see through, we tune out those magical messages. When we try to use our linear, logical mind to make decisions, drawing up lists of pros and cons, for instance, we forgo that sophisticated navigation system within us. Relying on logic to make our life's choices simply becomes a habit, and this habit causes confusion, cloudiness, and frustration. When we are constantly asking those around us for their advice, we get in the habit of not trusting what we know deep down. Deep down, we know what is going to nourish us, uplift us, and empower us. Yet it's difficult to access this knowing because it becomes buried or overlaid with mental constructs and limiting beliefs we have picked up along our trail.

In order to uncover this deep awareness, take a moment in quiet solitude to commune with your Spirit. When your monkey mind is running a hundred miles a minute, trying to figure out your best next step, you block out your natural instincts, which are always here to guide you. When you let go of the need to figure everything out, especially all at once, and you cease the need to know how everything is going to play out, your Spirit is enabled to step *in*. The ego mind wants to know, wants to analyze, so it can feel safe. Yet that larger part of you already resides in safety. It can see the larger puzzle or path, and it enjoys the journey as it unfolds.

The wise soul cares to be present with whatever is unfolding before her. The wise soul is dedicated to showing up in unconditional love, regardless of the circumstances. The conditioned ego is attached to *what* is happening and makes judgments about whether or not it likes it. The wise soul trusts that whatever is unfolding will inform his creative process. And so he is grateful and appreciative of whatever is presenting. He sees challenges as opportunities for his growth and leans in to face the situation at hand.

When we sit in present awareness with our soul, as our soul perspective, we become the witnesser, the observer of our life's unfolding. We become disentangled from what is happening around us—not disassociated, but unattached from the drama and details that would otherwise cause our ego mind to freak out or react or get triggered back into emotional trauma. As the witnesser, as the observer, we allow space between us and what's unfolding. This space allows us to respond rather than react, as we are more easily able to see the situation clearly through the eyes of neutrality.

The ego perspective cannot see the forest through the trees. Yet our soul perspective can see the trees and the forest and the surrounding areas around the forest. With this higher perspective, we can allow the drama and details, the hurts, the pains, to be healed or retuned naturally. Because from this higher vantage point, we no longer engage in the painful stories that we once thought were so true, so real for us. From this higher, more expanded lookout point, we can hold space for those parts of us that believed the nightmare was real. We can help these aspects to relax and loosen their grip on the painful perspectives, allowing them to return once again to the unified field where all is well, where all is One.

The ego learns to chase after what it *thinks* it needs for its survival, to be good enough or prove its worth. It learns to run away and avoid what it labels as painful or uncomfortable. Yet the soul sits with it all, faces it all, sees it all for what it truly is. Eventually, it becomes clear that there is nothing to run after, grasp for, to hide from, as those fearful perspectives were manifestations created from a scattered mind.

The wise soul leans back and allows life to support her. She gives space for life to unfold before her, knowing that life always brings her exactly what she needs. She remembers that the necessities for life are not extravagant or excessive, but simple, and she is grateful for this simplicity. To her, life is beautiful and abundant because of this. The wise soul knows what is truly important and makes these things priorities, whereas the ego grasps and seeks superficial or extravagant things it believes will bring it happiness. The wise soul knows that joy comes from within. The wise soul knows that she *is* joy.

Signs and Synchronicities

Your soul speaks to you in countless ways using signs and messages to help guide your way. This can be words that stand out to you in a song. It could be a conversation someone is having at the table next to you that piques your interest or answers a question that you've been asking. It could be through numbers that repeat themselves. It can simply be a gut feeling and you don't know why or how you know, but you simply know whether or not something is in your highest and best interest.

Learning to tune in to these messages, these seemingly magical signs, directs your focus back to your soul's guidance. When you lean into what is trying to communicate with you, you align more and more with magic, miracles, and synchronicities, which are natural and ever-present when you are paying attention. We tune them out when we are caught up in survival mentalities, fears, or other people's opinions. Giving yourself the time and space to hear, to see, to feel these divine messages will help make your journey smoother and much more enjoyable.

When you are truly paying attention, you realize that all of life is speaking to you, whether it's the insect that lands on your shoulder or the person in front of you who is speaking straight to your heart. The more we look for the messages designed into our experience, the more they reveal themselves. We can ask our Higher Self for signs, but we must be open and receptive, trusting that an answer will come. Our soul communicates using metaphors and symbology. You can use your intuition to decipher the meaning of anything that presents as significant to you. Your life is a treasure hunt filled with magical signs, and when you are present, you will discover these gifts everywhere you go.

If you're looking for true fulfillment, joy, ease, bliss, and beautiful, heaven-like experiences, you will find these in aligning to your soul's perspective; in doing the inner work to become a vibrational match to that of your soul. It's a process. It's a moment-by-moment choice. It takes dedication, it takes focus, and it takes surrender. And yet, when you walk this path, you begin to experience the true benefits and rewards that come from "work well done," that come from your devotion, and your efforts become clearly worthwhile.

You will feel the massive support behind you when you step out of your comfort zone and follow your inner guidance, which is always going to guide you to move toward unity, peace, harmony, collaboration. It's always going to guide you to support yourself, to support others, and to lean into the immense support all around you. Your Higher Self does not exist inside separation, so it never needs to compete with or try to win the attention of others in order to be happy. It's going to guide you to reach out and lend a helping hand from a place of true compassion, camaraderie, and Oneness, because the Higher Self knows; it remembers that the person in front of you *is* you.

When you dedicate yourself and your life to following your soul's guidance, you will notice a magical quality about things: synchronicities in the form of being in the right place at the right time, meeting those who are eager to support your higher vision, and resources flowing to you from unexpected sources appear and unfold all around you. In this surrendered state, you will find nothing is as it has appeared to be. All that you were taught will need to be surrendered and exchanged for higher understandings.

Others around you may not understand your soul's path—why you are choosing what you are choosing or sharing what you are called to share. Through your lens of ego, this will trigger all you've known yourself to be. Yet in moving through these challenges, you will come to find a freer and more expressive version of yourself. At some point, embodying your truth becomes of greater significance than what other people think about you.

DANIELLE KORT

Radiating your soul's truth is not a journey for the faint of heart. It takes patience and dedication to getting quiet, surrendering to presence, and to sitting with and facing all that has been unconscious. Following your soul's whisper is only uncomfortable because it has been silenced for so long, ignored, repressed, and seen as a foreign entity or even a figment of your imagination. Yet embracing the unknown is what you will be called to do in order to embody your soul and expand into all that you truly are. Your love is greater than any resistance coming from the ego mind, from the identities that you once thought you were.

Like a sandcastle that at one time appeared to be so sturdy and definitive will eventually be washed away by the warm, loving waters of the ocean, the identities you formed over and around your true essence will eventually come to be no more. And you, as an extension of All That Is, will reunite with this beautiful remembering. Call the ocean toward you with the intention of washing away all that you are not: the veils of illusion, the unconscious programming, the belief in separation. Know that there is a time and space for it all. And in divine timing, you, like everyone, will be washed and reclaimed back into the greater whole.

CHAPTER 5—DEDICATION TO AWAKENING

This journey of returning home to your true self, of transforming the shadow of unconsciousness into the light of universal awareness, requires doing your inner work. The call to do this work, to experience these transformations from within, doesn't often come because your life is easy and things are going well. This calling tends to come to you in the middle of the night when you're lying awake filled with anxieties, regrets, sorrow; when perhaps your life has become more stressful and unmanageable than you can handle; when you have been fired from your job, ended a thirty-year marriage, or your child has died unexpectedly. It is often the big challenges that push us to want to awaken from within, causing us to seek a solution, a higher way.

This calling can also come once you've gotten everything you *thought* would make you happy, yet you still find yourself unsatisfied, lost, unfulfilled. It is in this moment that you think to yourself, *There's got to be more!* This drive to find a deeper meaning in life catalyzes our evolution. It starts us on this path of conscious awakening.

When you know your "why," your reason for pursuing this inner journey, it sustains your hunger to expand beyond what you have known to be true. Soul growth happens not only *to* you but *through* you with your active participation. When you are truly ready to move out of the painful perspectives, limitations, and suffering and reignite your innate joy and passion, you automatically call to you supportive forces that will guide your way into the light. When you've finally had enough of superficial and meaningless exchanges and you surrender to your desire for closer connections from the heart, everything that was in your way of this shall be shown to you. And with your intention and recognition, it will be removed.

Sometimes the dream of a unified, harmonious, and peaceful existence is all we need to inspire us to this transformation from within. Whatever your "why," know that your soul's journey is perfectly designed to activate your evolutionary path. When things are going well, we might be tempted to plateau at a certain place of understanding, yet the calling for soul growth is never-ending. When we try to keep things just the way they are, life will show us that nothing is meant to be permanent, and all things will be made new once they have completed their purpose. Change is inevitable, and soul growth is the reason you are here.

When we are fully present with the people and experiences in our life, in our dream, knowing that these moments are so very precious and won't last forever, we are enlivened to live even more fully. There is a purpose to the seasons of our life, and when we can embrace the impending changes, we are led through extraordinary adventures. The soul is adventurous at its core. When you surrender to the inner and outer explorations of this vast experience beyond words, your adventurous spirit becomes impassioned once again, and life becomes a joyous journey filled with freedoms that were once unimaginable.

When we try to control the people, experiences, and landscapes of our outer reflections, life will reveal how we're only holding ourselves back. It is only the identities we have believed we are that see growth as a threat, as the scary unknown that should be avoided at all costs. Yet our Higher Self will always guide us to see beyond the fear and expand into new territories where we can free ourselves further from these old constructs. When we listen from within and follow this guidance, things become smoother and more enjoyable. It takes trust, courage, and faith to move beyond what we've known. Yet when we do move through that fear, we are greeted on the other side with divine compensation for work well done.

The Choice to Surrender

Here is a question to ask yourself: Will you allow your spiritual evolution to be smooth and gentle or will you cause it to be harsh and bumpy? The more you resist, the harder it becomes. The more you try to control with your linear mind, the tougher and rougher the experience. The more you let go and surrender, even free-falling into your own awakening as you allow your Spirit to guide you, the softer and smoother the experience becomes.

There is no right or wrong in any of our choices, yet we always have a choice. You will inevitably awaken, yet you have the choice to do so willingly or unwillingly. It's a freewill universe. You get to choose how you would like to direct your will. Will you resist your awakening, your inner guidance, or will you flow with it? Cooperate with it? Team up with it?

If we don't clear the dense energies, such as resentment, traumatic memories, and grief, they build up like a kind of energetic plaque. These dense energies cloud our perception. With the assistance and guidance of our Higher Self, we are constantly being presented with the opportunity to clear away the fog, the forgetfulness, the overlays, the veils, the protective mechanisms, the ego identities that have kept us seeing through a cloudy perspective and walking through a dull, murky dream.

So the question remains: Will you take up these opportunities and choose to participate in this clearing and soul re-emergence process, or will you kick and scream and resist, giving your Spirit/Soul/Higher Self no other choice but to "shake you loose" from your attachments to old, outmoded ways (which is the not-so-fun route)? We might see this as "being hit over the head with a two-by-four" when you don't listen to your intuition or inner guidance. In choosing to resist, your Higher Self has to make things uncomfortable enough so that you are forced to let go and surrender to your ascension process, forced to prioritize it.

Often, when we know it's time to make a big life change, we ignore this inner knowing because we're scared of the unknown and we don't want to leave behind the routine, location, or people we've become so comfortable with, even if it's a toxic situation. The inspiration for this change comes from your inner guidance, and the resistance comes from your ego. When you resist, eventually your Higher Self arranges for your "bottle to be taken away" when it's time for you to graduate to a sippy cup. The ego identity doesn't like this and sees it as a loss when, really, it's a graduation into the next level of your life.

Let's say you've worked as an accountant for over a decade, crunching numbers and generating countless stacks of spreadsheets. You've become quite proficient, but the truth is you're bored to tears. Within the last few years, a new passion for the healing arts has emerged inside you. You've now taken classes, received several certifications, and even gotten your license to be a professional masseuse and energy healer. It has only been a far-off fantasy to become a full-time massage therapist, even though you are attracting a nice flow of clients on the side.

You have received the inner guidance, again and again, to make space in your calendar so you can receive a greater number of clients who would benefit from your energetic healing and touch. Yet you avoid this guidance because you're afraid to leave behind the security of your biweekly paycheck. Eventually, your Higher Self steps forward on your behalf. It removes the distraction, which had once served a purpose but now stands in the way of your new fulfilling career, which is ready to be integrated into your life in a bigger way. To your shock and dismay, you get fired from your accounting job. And while your ego might see this as loss or rejection, it was your Higher Self "pulling the trigger" on your behalf, creating space in your schedule so that your most current passions could take center stage.

When you are actively dedicated to your soul's path, you can intuitively feel when it's time to switch from the bottle to the sippy cup and from the sippy cup to the drinking glass. Not only do you hear the guidance, but you take the initiative and follow it. You don't plug your ears and say, "Nah nah nah," pretending you don't hear it. You don't say, "I don't wanna!" and you don't judge the impending change that obviously needs to be made. You simply make the change without having to be forced. The transition is smooth for you because of this. It's softer, gentler, and much more satisfying.

Rather than being dragged through your ascension journey, you can get *ahead* of things. When you partner with your Higher Self, you begin taking responsibility for your life, you initiate your healing, your integration, your activations. You choose to become the observer *now*. You get curious about the reflections, manifestations, or life circumstances before you without judging them, without becoming victimized by them. Instead, you become empowered by your outer world reflections, because you see them as opportunities to better understand and grow in your creative capacities.

Your soul is here to grow. Your ego resists this growth because it feels scary and threatening to its perceived safety and comfortability. Yet the choice remains yours. Indulge your ego, continue the sagas, tantrums, and dramas, *or* ... choose anew.

Birthing Your Soul's Expression

Take a moment to ask yourself these questions: What have I been devoting my time, energy, and attention to? Have I been more focused on the dramas of the outer world, giving in to fear or my ego fantasies? Or have I been deeply devoted to my soul's inner quest for freedom and expansion, to a deepening of presence and joy? We can make a new choice in every moment with each new breath we take. When we reflect upon our previous choices with neutrality and compassion, we can make more soul-aligned choices with this new awareness.

The journey of awakening to your true self comes with challenges, yet these challenges present themselves to shake things up and allow you to expand into greater possibilities. If you choose to consciously participate in what wants to naturally occur through you, you open to a much more gratifying and pleasurable process of ascension. To embark on this journey with your deepest devotion is to honor this gift of life in the most profound and beautiful way. Walking the path of the soul is for those who crave a deeper intimacy with themselves and others. It is for those who desire more fun and inspiring surprises and who dare to dance with the mysteries of life. This path is equally for those who want to realize their true potential, be their fullest expression, and fulfill their soul's mission at the top of their genius. If any of this describes you, then you are ready for this journey of soul emergence.

Soul emergence, leading into soul embodiment, is a moment-by-moment process, as you are continually weaving in greater awareness, which is required to sense and follow your inner guidance. When we operate from the limitations of our ego identities, we often want to hide from our inner guidance. We want to pretend we can't hear it. We fear what it is calling us toward. Yet the fear only exists in our clouded perception. Our Higher Self, however, is feeling the excitement of what is next for us. It's thrilled to help us switch it up, feeling that expansion being birthed from within us.

When you really tune in and listen, you know what there is for you to feel, express, and transform from within. You know what inspired action there is for you to take. We can only lie to ourselves so long before we get sick of the lies. We can paint it every which way, pretending we don't want what our soul is calling us toward. We can continue to play small and resist the inevitable energy that wants to flow through us, the inevitable dreams of our Spirit. Yet we'd only be holding ourselves back from the beauty and awe of what wants to be birthed from our soul.

Fears can and do come up for a woman preparing to give birth. It's normal and it's okay. But does that woman allow the fear to stop her from showing up on the day she's ready to deliver her beautiful newborn baby? The more she resists in fear, the more painful that birth is. The more she surrenders to what is natural, what wants to naturally occur through her body, through her being, the easier and smoother that birth is.

You, too, have many, many gifts that want to be expressed, want to be birthed and shared with others. This is your innate birthright. It is your divine right to experience the joy that comes from your beautiful and unique expression. It is only you who can resist and try to stuff away that creative expression due to your doubts and fears, worries and concerns. You can look in every direction, trying to find the escape route, trying to avoid your very expression, but inevitably, the light within you will shine through. Deep down you want this. And so it is truly a process of surrendering to that larger part of you, to that deepest spark within you.

What is your song that wants to be sung? How does it sound? What does it feel like? It's very different from anything you've heard before. It's unfamiliar and yet so in tune with your soul. It is only unfamiliar to the conditioned mind, which has made up stories that say it's unsafe to be who and what you truly are, to express your innate gifts with exuberant joy. It's the conditional mind that says others will judge me or be jealous of me or try to compete with me, so why try in the first place? These are the things that hold us back, that stop us from getting out of our own way.

We can surrender these fears, these limiting stories, and return to dedicating ourselves to our soul's continual growth. These are slight shifts we can make in each moment. When we fall back into the old rut of the limited ways we had been perceiving, we can simply move our consciousness out of the rut and back into that alignment of what we know to be true deep within us. We can know and remember that we are completely safe and validated in expressing our divine essence. Returning to this safety is a process of remembering and affirming this deep knowing again and again until the reflections of your life's dream physically demonstrate this remembrance.

As you evolve and experience life through the lens of trust and flow, every cell of your body begins to feel safe. Remembering that you are safe allows your inner creative gifts to come forward and be expressed fully, freely, and passionately. You must want this from the core of your being, to make those internal shifts again and again, no matter what is occurring "out there," no matter what is unfolding before you. It will require your ability to soothe yourself, to coo yourself through the pain, to breathe through the fear. It will require your dedication to living in a world filled with peace, compassion, joy, and unlimited possibilities. This is something you want, you desire, from deep inside of you.

When you show up to meet yourself in every experience, nothing can stop you from aligning to this reality. When your soul's emergence, your divine expression, your heart's fulfillment, becomes your top priority, you move well along your path toward freedom, toward enlightenment. Be still and know that you are immensely supported, guided, and loved along this journey of awakening and remembering.

The Priorities of Your Spirit

We can get so caught up in our daily agendas and to-do lists that we don't *think* we have time for anything else. When you really step back and look at your life from a more expanded view, it becomes easier to see how you've been spending your time and energy and what you've been prioritizing. Let's say you've had the desire to paint simply for the joy and expression you feel by bringing color to canvas. Or perhaps you've been meaning to take a bubble bath so that you can relax and unwind, but you never seem to find the time. Instead, you find yourself consumed with work-related tasks and household chores, or maybe you're wrapped up in a relationship where you don't want to leave your partner's side. The important thing to note is that you always have a choice as to how you spend your time and energy.

It is actually in slowing down that you can gain more time, as you are the one who speeds it up when you're running a hundred miles per minute. If you believe there's never enough time, take a guess at what you're creating for your experience. When we prioritize these inclinations of the soul, like our creative pursuits and our methods of relaxation and rejuvenation, we feed our soul and that light within us grows stronger. This doesn't mean that we have to set aside our to-do lists completely, but it's imperative that we take time out to reconnect with our beautiful Spirit. The more we honor our inner callings, the more we fall into place with our divine blueprint, our sacred soul's destiny.

Take some time and space now to reflect on what fills your schedule or gets most of your attention. What have you been prioritizing up to this point? Then ask yourself these questions: Where am I coming from when I deem these things worthy of my time and effort? Is this thing that I think is so important stemming from fear or love? From lack or a passion for creation? Asking yourself these questions will help clarify your true wants and desires versus what you think you *have* to do because of fear or survival programming. Return to the present moment, this moment right here, and feel in your higher heart which life priorities feel highest or most aligned. You can assess your priorities regularly and continue to make your soul guidance number one.

There is so much going on in the outer world that it's easy to lose sight of what's truly important. The pursuit of money for the sake of getting rich or the drive for power or status serves as a distraction from walking your soul's path. Focusing solely on your family's needs or shortcomings rather than looking in the mirror to see what needs your attention or binge-watching Netflix instead of making space to explore your newest interests or passions—these habits hinder your evolution as a soul.

In the big picture, it's actually harder to stay distracted. It's harder to avoid presence, harder to avoid walking your soul's path. So surrender the drama, the fear, the upset. Surrender your reactions to "out there" and come back here, right here, to this ever-present miracle. You remember this feeling. It has always been here within you, and it always will be.

Let go of your need to control and instead surrender to the divine design that wants to be birthed through you, by you, with you. Be there for you. Be here for you. Betray no one, especially yourself. Be a true friend to yourself, and dedicate yourself to the courageous act of self-love, which is the awakening of your Spirit from within you.

Heartfelt Dedication

Life does not get better by chance; it gets better with change, with transformation. What is ready to be transformed from within you? When you feel stuck or blocked, it is only because you are seeing through the lens of one perspective. There are a multitude of perspectives and ways of looking at something.

You can look at your life experiences as stories and extract the drama out of them; you can cling to the identity you've created because of that experience you had; you can create fantastical tales about why you are limited or lacking or unlovable. Or ... you can see the experience through the eyes of neutrality, observing the *dynamics* that lent a hand to a very important lesson you learned. You can extract the gold from the situation, distilling the higher wisdom gleaned from that situation, and you will expand your consciousness in the process. The other choice is to hold on to feelings of suffering and separation from a past that you carry with you. One comes from the soul's quest for freedom, the other comes from the ego's addiction to drama. One unchains you from the density, suffering, and limitations you have known, the other keeps you playing them out. How you choose to go about your life's journey is always up to you. It's always a choice.

The choice for higher, lighter, and brighter experiences, when it is exercised regularly with heartfelt dedication, eventually turns into embodiment. It becomes natural to follow your soul guidance and choose your highest alignment. Eventually, there is no choice because soul embodiment becomes your highest priority. It becomes your way of life and the love of your life. You embody your soul so veraciously, so passionately, that you flow with the wind and dance with the stars and sing with the birds, and you chuckle that there once was a time when you questioned the exquisite song of your soul.

CHAPTER 6—TEARS OF GRATITUDE

If only life were easier. This is a thought that so many of us have had. You might picture yourself on a remote tropical island with an umbrella drink in hand as you ponder what it would be like to get away from the problems of your everyday life. But have you ever considered what a month or a year of this same daily activity would be like? There's no doubt that stagnation or boredom would become quite present.

So while this might *sound* like a nice way to spend all your days, it lacks the true purpose for your soul's incarnation. If we never experienced challenges or contrast from our desires, we would never grow into all that we came here to be. Pleasure is a wonderful experience, but when there is no purpose or soul fulfillment to be found, it leaves our lives feeling flat or surface-level. As we answer the calling to go deeper and expand our hearts and minds into possibilities we never previously imagined, our soul becomes enlivened, and the quality of our lives becomes enriched.

We may look at someone who's led a very easy life. He was fed with a silver spoon and handed everything he ever wanted since the day he was born. He never had to work or go past his comfortable limits, so he doesn't know what he has. Then look at someone who was drafted into the military, fought for years, and then finally returns home to his family. The experience of coming home is truly joyous, and tears of gratitude roll down his cheeks because he knows just how good he has it with his family, living in love rather than warring in violence and fighting to earn his living.

We, too, are coming home. The immense joy bubbling up within each person choosing this homecoming experience is beyond words, beyond comprehension. The experience is over-joyous, unfathomable, and rapturous for all beings, not only on this earth plane but beyond this planet, throughout the solar systems, throughout the universe. It can be felt. Each of us is coming back home, back online, back to this Oneness and connectedness to the unified field; back to this ever-present, overflowing joy that runs through this interconnected web and intrinsically links us.

This *one* pulsing heartbeat gets to be felt and experienced by each of us as we awaken from our slumber, and this pulse is beyond magnificent. Our gratitude for *this* experience amplifies, and this sensation cannot be described in words. A ticket for this ride we call life is priceless, and when we stop judging our experience, letting that film or overlay fall away, we can see clearly that this is a beautiful, wondrous, heavenly, joyous experience. And so, it is time for us to clear the cobwebs, open the blinds, and ease our way back into the light, back into our truth, where gratitude for what is ripens into our everyday experience; where this appreciation becomes something we no longer have to work at.

Here, we exist in deep reverence for all of life, for all of our existences, for all of our experiences, knowing that all experiences have added to our growth, to the expansion of the universe, and that nothing has been done in vain. To find ourselves here, we intentionally practice the vibration of gratitude, eventually remembering that it's been our truth all along. We see that we've only temporarily journeyed away from our Source (perspective-wise) for a purposeful experience. When we return to seeing through the eyes of gratitude, we see clearly. This means being tuned in to your heart, following your heart, choosing from and honoring your heart, choice by choice and moment by moment.

Removing Judgment and Ego Expectations

It can be challenging to have an attitude of gratitude when our predominant thoughts stem from judgment. The resentments, the chips on on your shoulder, the on-going frustrations in your life all result from judgment: judging what is, judging what has been, and judging others for their part in this experience that you've labeled as not good enough, bad, wrong. Yet everything is happening *for* you, not to you. You are not a victim of circumstance.

Appreciation naturally arises when we open our heart and return to the present moment. When we pick ourselves apart, curse our experience, or blame the one before us, we are coming from limited perception, from the ego mind's viewpoint. We are closing off that natural connection to Source as we tighten our grip of (perceived) control. We are cutting ourselves off from those people or parts of us that we reject. It is a lens that we are choosing to see through.

We can choose to see our world as ugly, hostile, and as a threat to our safety, which we must neurotically protect ourselves from. Yet the more we do this, the more this type of world presents itself in our outer reflections. When we open our heart, the floodgates of ancient wisdom spill forth and remind us of what has always been true within us. When we encounter an experience that we do not prefer, it might feel familiar to fall victim to it, feeling like it shouldn't be happening. The key, however, is to face what is presenting before you and choose to bring greater awareness to it, seeing the larger picture and uplifting your perception to this higher state of consciousness; allowing that timeless part of you to help mend or shift those perspectives that are based in pain, confusion, hurt.

Imagine you're getting married and your big day is right around the corner. You put much preparation into what will be an extravagant and costly affair. When your wedding day finally arrives, you expect it to be the best day of your life. But after your nails have been painted and hair curled to perfection, you find out that your soon-to-be husband is nowhere to be found. With a crowd of family and friends who have highly anticipated this momentous occasion already seated and awaiting the ceremony, you can't seem to accept the reality of this situation. *How could this be happening to me right now?!*

The wedding is called off because you discover that your ex-fiancé got cold feet. This day you had dreamt of since you were a little girl now feels like a nightmare you wish wasn't real. Your mind kicks into overdrive as you go over that day again and again, wondering what you could have done differently to avoid this embarrassing and painful experience.

When you find yourself in this kind of situation, rather than holding on to the painful perspective or trying to shift it from the same level of consciousness or understanding it was created from, you can simply surrender the pain to that larger part of you, to God Source Consciousness or the Universe. You don't need to know the solution (at least not right away) in order for it to be healed. Just relax and let go. Surrender your need to fix or fight or run away from it. Give yourself the space and time to step away from the drama and details of what happened and return to the safety inside your heart. From here, clear guidance for healing can and will reveal itself in divine right timing.

This clarity could come within moments of taking a breath and stepping back, or it might take years. Resting inside the sanctuary of your pure high heart and allowing that knowing to come forward and reveal itself in its divine timing helps you to untangle from the pain. That knowing or clarity might nudge you to have an honest conversation with those you're dealing with, or perhaps it guides you to drop the situation altogether and keep moving forward. You can trust that each situation presents itself as an opportunity for your growth and your ability to refine your creational process. Nothing happens by chance, and when you take total responsibility for your part in what transpired, knowing that it all happened *for* you, not *to* you, then you no longer feel helpless on your journey. Instead, you feel empowered to make a new choice from a broader perspective and watch that inner shift ripple into your physical reality.

Let's say your ex-fiancé in the previous example has officially chosen to go his own way. For weeks you're filled with regret, despair, disappointment, and agony over what took place, and your mind runs in circles wishing you could change what happened. One morning, though, you have the inspiration to go for a jog, which you haven't done in years. As you're running, you feel spaciousness from the situation, and you feel guided to surrender this pain to the Universe/God Source/your Higher Self. You make a morning jog part of your new routine because here you can get out of your head and open to the larger picture.

Eventually, you're able to clearly see that you had been spending every waking moment with your ex-fiancé and no time on your own passions and purpose. You're able to admit that deep down, you knew accepting that wedding proposal was not in your highest alignment. You now know that your friends and family don't care about that wedding day; they just want to see you happy. On one of your morning jogs, the inspiration to pick up that manuscript you had started writing years ago hits you like a strike of lightning. So you work passionately day in and day out to complete this book, and the published project becomes wildly successful. This new zest for life allows you to look back and see in retrospect that this previously painful experience was actually a blessing in disguise.

Rather than dwelling on a challenging experience from the lens of your pain-filled persona, you can open up to a higher understanding by giving that pain to God. With a clear mind and an open heart, exchange your painful perspective for greater awareness, allowing new life to emerge. Instead of remaining upset about what has occurred or holding resentment toward those around you, take a moment to reflect by looking within yourself, When perhaps did I ignore the whisper of my soul before this challenging event transpired? Where might I be harboring bitterness or an unwillingness to forgive, which is blocking me from moving forward with a new sense of purpose, passion, or drive? What emotional trauma might need to be tended to so that I may experience this person or situation in a new light? With a simple reattunement of our energy, we can free ourselves from the victimhood, judgments, and ego expectations that had kept us interpreting our experience as painful. When we remember that all things can be made new, we naturally appreciate the creative freedoms that we have as physical expressions of the Divine.

Each experience is here to show you how you create and how you can grow in your creative abilities. Whether consciously or unconsciously, you manifest through the power of your thoughts and emotions, by your outwardly expressed actions and your choices. This miracle of manifestation is something we can be incredibly grateful for because we get to interact in a physical way with that which we creatively concoct from within, like an inventor who gets to revel in the deliciousness of her or his invention once it's been created. You get to rendezvous with others who mirror back to you where you've been vibrationally and see if that's something you want to continue or transform.

Appreciation is a connector to, a tool for, and a result of alignment. Judgment or cursing, belittling, putting yourself and others down—these are ways to disconnect and create more fragmentation, more separation. When we judge others, ourselves, and our dream as "not good enough," we cause resistance inside of us and upheaval "out there." Our perception fragments further.

When we can remember that everything happens for a reason and nothing happens by chance, we can relax back into trusting in the divine design of our life's dream. Rest assured that the words coming out of your mouth, the songs being played on the radio, the people coming into your reality are all here to show you something. Nothing is a coincidence, and all things present themselves as an opportunity for your greatest growth and creative mastery. Relax into that, trust in that, breath in the peace of *that*. It's happening *for* you, *through* you, not *to* you. Ultimately, every breath is growth, as you are continually moving up a spiral of evolution. Even the nightmares or contrasting experiences are part of your ever-unfolding expansion.

Surrendering Control of the Ego

What if you relinquished your need to know if that person you're dating is the one you'll be with for the rest of your life? What if you were simply present in the relationship, choosing to open your heart anyway and love, just as you would like to show up in love with all people you meet? Hurt only comes from lack of clear, honest, and open-hearted communication. It comes from a separation mentality. You cannot be hurt if you do not attach yourself to people, situations, or places.

Go with the flow of your Spirit, enjoy what and who is in front of you fully in the moment, and let go of the need to label or define what will happen next. Hold your desires and visions without attachment, knowing that they can and will manifest if they are in vibrational resonance with you, and they will manifest in divine right timing. It may not happen the way you imagine or with the person you think it will be with, but when you relax and trust your life's unfolding, knowing that it is happening perfectly for you, then you can remain in the present moment without getting caught up in the conceptualizations of your mind. When you are in the small mind, you are not present. When you drop back into your heart and show up in the fullness of what and who you truly are, you can enjoy life to the fullest. When you allow a fearful mind to run the show, you cut yourself off from this full experience.

So be here now. Trust that all you need is within you and unfolding before you in divinely perfect timing. Discern whether you would like to meet the situation at hand with the old paradigm it was created from or if you're ready to see it through the eyes of unconditional love and neutrality, from the higher perspective of your soul, the observer. When you choose the latter, you automatically find resolve with the details and dramas of your past.

The Effects of Polarity and Neutrality

We are constantly molding and shaping our reality, moment by moment, based on our choices, and this is done on both an individual and collective level. Our diverse experiences naturally cause friction which propels us to contemplate reality, evolving our belief systems and ultimately expanding us into greater awareness.

Polarity, light and dark, was originally designed so you could choose your own adventures based on your preferences, but because of where collective consciousness has been steered by a desire for power and control, polarity has become skewed into discordance. Constant judgment is what fuels this discordance. While one person may not gravitate toward darkness, another individual may prefer to explore it, and there need be no judgment about this.

Darkness does not need to be labeled "evil" or "villain." The more we judge the one before us as being bad, wrong, or worse than and the more we fight against or reject the other, the more we are fueling the very thing we do not prefer. There is no need to fight darkness with light or take sides in a combative manner. When you hold two sides of the same spectrum in opposition, believing that one is right and the other wrong, this polarizing perspective holds you in a dualistic purgatory. As we remove our judgment of others' choices—their political parties, choice of diet, religious or spiritual preference—we allow light and dark to find some common ground within our own consciousness.

Returning to neutrality can help us transform any confronting experience into its higher expression. Neutrality is not about being despondent or feeling powerless. Choosing neutrality, or the middle road, is releasing our judgment about specific choices or preferences, relinquishing our need to be right or another to be different than they are.

We do not see sleeping as "bad" or being awake as "good," nor is light better than darkness (or vice versa); again they exist on a spectrum where one is dimmer and the other brighter. Darkness represents unconsciousness or less awareness. Light represents greater awareness. The "shadows" within us are simply parts of us that we have repressed or rejected. We can repress parts of us that act from pain or fear, just as we can repress our light, or that most authentic, brilliant version of us. As we grow our awareness and shine it lovingly on our shadows, it's like flipping on a light switch in a dark room—suddenly the darkness is gone. Unconsciousness becomes conscious. As we remove the judgment of what we have repressed or rejected, holding it in a space of compassionate grace, we emerge from the dark corner where we had been hiding.

Aligning to New Earth

Allow yourself to remember your divine birthright to true freedom, full expression, soul-alignment, interactions that light you up, and that match your internal joy. As you embody an alignment of mind, body, spirit, heart, the worries and concerns, fears and resistance fall to the wayside. When your field has been cleared and you reside in this space of unconditional love, you see clearly. You feel light and effervescent. You move with fluidity, purpose, exuberance. You love deeply, and you are intimate with all of life. Because, in this space, there is nothing to fear, fight against, prove, defend, or justify.

Here, you exist upon New Earth, a harmonious world built from the roots of integrity, honesty, and respect. You move with the energy that creates worlds. You flow this energy through you. You work in harmony with this energy. You remember that you are one with the ocean, rather than trying to separate yourself as a drop, rather than trying to push the ocean in the direction your mind *thinks* it should be going. Instead, you surrender, you relax into that unified network, that field of Unity Consciousness, where you reside in total safety and ease.

Here, you have a deep appreciation for life, for existence, for all experiences, because here you trust once again. When you trust in the support that is always surrounding you beyond the illusion of separation, when you trust in your Higher Self that is always guiding you beyond your attempts to shut it out, when you trust in the divine design of your waking dream, you begin opting out of the struggle and the judgments that kept you separate from experience itself—from the experience that is *you*. When you stop running from yourself, hiding from yourself, segmenting yourself, compartmentalizing yourself, compartmentalizing All That Is, you come back *home* to yourself. You come back home to the experience of *Oneness*.

Start by dipping your toe into the warm waters of unconditional love. Feel in your body how this feels to no longer judge the conditions of your life, of your dream, to no longer need conditions to be what you *think* they should be from the lens of ego. Notice what it feels like to put down the burdens, to set down the heavy baggage of judgment and control. Your need to control keeps you stuck—running in circles, trying so very hard to keep it all together. But these false premises are *meant* to fall apart, to break down, and to no longer control *you*.

All that was built upon unsteady foundations are meant to crumble. The systems you have known "out there" that were built with these dense intentions and energetics will fall like a house of cards. And this is for your highest evolution, for the highest evolution of all, *for* this awakening to occur. This false premise that you need to control your dream from a place of fear, from a place of lack or scarcity, from a place of struggle or striving, or even that you need to control at all—this is not based in universal truth. It was only a fear-based idea, a belief.

Many fear that if they let go, their life will turn into chaos. But when you let go of control, the control of your ego mind, that is when your Higher Self can step in and guide you, and your divine destiny comes to the forefront. Open your heart and open your mind to possibilities that you may never have imagined. Open yourself to the magic and the miracles that exist right here.

Surrender the veils of illusion, the overlays of untruths, the fear that you're a slave to a system that puts your needs last. Let go of the lies and illusions that permeate the 3D systems of control. These systems are a macrocosm of the microcosms of control within us. As you surrender the control of your ego, you can pull out of the matrixes of control "out there." As you surrender to your higher consciousness, you become a vibrational match to a unified grid of light created for and in service to the greater good of all.

Equality, honor, respect, integrity, and clear, open, honest communication is your new normal upon New Earth in this new era where conscious awareness reigns supreme. Feel your heart blossoming and opening to this new alignment. Ask yourself, Do the greed, manipulation, and lies still feel true? If so, then ask yourself, Am I ready and willing to let this go? They were only a practiced vibration, a thought you kept thinking which became a belief, and these beliefs created a belief system that projected your life's dream "out there."

In tuning our antenna to the channel of loving awareness, all that we once thought was reality reveals itself to be the programming of an entertainment guide created by a fearful persona. We can retune our focus and open our heart to an experience of gratitude at a moment's notice. We are our own channel changers, and we can opt out of the fearful scripts that were written from pain and suffering. The freedoms we have to create our experience can be exceptionally blissful when we exercise them. Our empowerment paves the way for a grateful heart, and a grateful heart reunites us with the empowered Creator within.

Trusting in Your Divine Design

Start with the seed of unity. Water it with the intention of unifying all aspects of you, then all beings, all planets, all universes. Knowing that, yes, your individuality is a beautiful part of this experience in a physical body, and you get to express yourself in unique and brilliant ways, all while simultaneously embodying this connection to All That Is. Tuning in from these different vantage points as you merge and integrate them... what joy it is! What a beautiful, precious experience this life and ascension journey is.

Trust in the unfoldment of your life, of your dream, of your interactions. Trust that your reflections will always show you, inform you, about your creative choices and where you have been creating from. Then use that feedback to continue aligning, tweaking, activating, surrendering, and clearing from within. In the old system you might have thought you needed to build an empire, self-made, striving, going it alone, but to enter New Earth, it's truly about letting all of that go.

All you were taught, born of the ego, is here to fall away now, and what you surrender to is your Higher Self, God, Source, the Universe... is this divine design, this harmonic orchestra which orchestrates beautiful assemblies, experiences, and connections. Feel into the wonderment of that! The beauty and awe in that! The mystery of that!

The attitude that "everything is always working out for my highest good. Thank you!" tunes you back into that flow, that ease, that way of working *with* the universal energies. Because it *is* always truly working out for you in wondrous ways. It is only the ego that judges it and then tunes into the perception that has us thinking things and people are against us, cutting us out, causing us harm, laughing at us, out to get us. It only takes a simple tuning, like a tuning fork, tuning your vibration and tuning it back to appreciation.

As you practice the vibration of appreciation more and more, it becomes your new normal, and you drop the density—that ego resistance, that judgment—not *needing* things to be different, yet knowing that as you tune by universal law, everything changes. You shift to a different vibrational and dimensional experience—moment by moment, choice by choice—to focus on lighter and brighter thoughts and feelings. Tune your instrument to come back into harmony with the universal orchestra, where things just feel and sound so much more exquisite, epic, wondrous, divine!

Forgiving What Happened

The most painful and triggering experiences can be the catalysts we need for our greatest growth. The key is to open your heart, even when your smaller self would like to close it and protect you from potential future pain. We can open our heart by forgiving those who we perceive have hurt us. Forgiveness is a graceful gift we give to ourselves and others. It is a way that we let go of the poison we have been carrying around.

That poison is comprised of the grievances, resentments, and bitterness we hold in our energetic and physical bodies. It dims our light and toxifies our cellular structure. It blocks us from developing deeply rooted relationships and weighs us down with its density. When we look closer at forgiveness, we can see that it is really a willingness to let go of the judgment we had placed upon an interaction or situation. Had we never judged the situation in the first place, forgiveness would not even be necessary.

If we can truly accept that all circumstances are here for our greatest growth, then we can flow with grace through any situation. This realization may take some time to settle into your awareness. The more you allow this understanding to reveal itself, that life is *for* you and not against you, the easier it becomes to face whatever is unfolding, receive the gift within it and expand beyond any old, perceived limitations that had once caused you pain or suffering. Suffering is a choice. It is a lens that we choose to see through. It is not bad or wrong; it is simply limiting.

When you reach the point where you can feel gratitude toward the person who you felt hurt you, you have come to a place of complete forgiveness. You have taken your power back. You have reclaimed your life force energy. You have chosen to open your heart.

Those who you interact with and play out certain dynamics with signed a soul contract with you agreeing to play a role that would help further your growth. They raised their hand to be, perhaps, your greatest teacher. And you can know that these momentary experiences are but exercises or lessons for you to learn from, ways that you challenge yourself to choose unconditional love over fearful and painful perspectives. While it might have felt like this person broke your heart, what they were actually doing was acting as a symbol *for your heart to break open*, catalyzing your expansion.

If you lost a child, for instance, you might be angry at God, the Universe, yourself, or even the child. You might be focused on the loss or the pain, yet this experience brings many gifts. Maybe it allowed you to live more in the present, realizing that your life experience is so very precious and can come to an end in any moment. Perhaps it is here to show you that you are eternal and that the Spirit of your child lives on, that they have moved beyond the human experience and back into Unity Consciousness, where they now reside in unconditional peace and love. Maybe you begin to tune in to their presence, which does not need a physical body, and they now become a guiding light or guardian angel for you. Even though the situation can feel painful, it can also expand your perception to new realizations, ultimately opening you to greater love than you have previously known. When we allow life to guide us along our evolutionary path, trusting in its divine orchestration, we loosen our grip on the density, the pain, the anxieties, the resentments, and we free ourselves more and more.

It's common to allow a tough situation to tear you up inside, but you cannot manifest or align to a new desired reality until you accept what is and what has been. As soon as you find peace with how things have gone and with things you cannot control, a situation you might have considered irreparable can now loosen and rearrange itself in seemingly miraculous ways. By accepting where you stand today and even appreciating your life's challenges, that is when a new day starts to dawn.

When you are immersed fully in a state of appreciation where you allow each of life's intricacies to bend and flow, shape and create your ever-unfolding experience, you revel in the deliciousness of that which is here to guide your way. You trust that your footing is secure and your desire to create courageously is enhanced. You act from a place of willingness to expand beyond the limitations you have known. Your heart is open, so you trust that all you will ever need will unfold before you in the timing required for your highest well-being. Because you appreciate rather than condemn, you stay open to the miracles of life that are waiting for you to meet them. A life we can be grateful for reveals itself when we are grateful for the life we are already living.

CHAPTER 7—BURSTS OF JOY

To enjoy your life is to honor your Spirit and the Spirit of Creation itself. Fear, separation, heartache have all been purposeful teaching aids to help us appreciate and enjoy our experience more deeply. Take a moment and notice what sensations cause you to feel joy. Notice the places where you feel unsafe to feel joy and choose instead to trust your joy. Like a long-lost friend, joy wants to be reintroduced into your experience in a more intimate way than you have known before. Joy, like all emotions, all feelings, all sensations, is valid.

Joy comes naturally when you learn to surrender the burdens, the struggles, the pressures, the resistance. It comes naturally when you come back to the present moment. You can also align with joy by learning to focus on what causes you to feel joy. What lights you up? What impassions you?

Joy cannot be lost, but you can cut yourself off from joy. Joy is your Spirit wanting to emerge and flow through you from within. It wants to be shared with others. This deepest part of you wants joy for all. It is only the parts of you in pain that want to be accompanied by others in pain. Yet when we allow joy to take center stage, letting our Spirit flow freely, we detach from that pain. We shift out of it.

We can have the deepest compassion for that pain, but we don't need to wallow in it. We can allow our compassion to transform that pain, and we can focus on our joyful Spirit, our Spirit that is free of the limited programming, conditioning, and fearful thoughts that have previously run us. Now we can choose to allow *joy* to guide us. Although it may seem like suffering is just the way of the world, we truly came here to live and play in joy. The more you allow yourself to experience joy, the lighter you will feel. Ascending out of the denser frequencies and into lighter frequencies such as joy is what ascension is all about.

As we let go of those dense thoughts and emotions, we lighten our load. We ascend back into our innate, ever-present experience of joy. As we allow ourselves to be moved by joy, we give others permission to do the same. We can allow our joy to flow out from within us and into others' experiences. Just a simple heartfelt smile can make someone else's day. You may not be aware of the magnitude of this effect, but deep down you know that it is potent and powerful. Our joy can heal the world, but first, we focus on allowing it to heal each of us individually.

You can imagine joy as a brilliant sun radiating from the core of your being. This light expands as you allow more and more joy to radiate out from within you. Without needing conditions "out there" to make you happy, you can choose joy right now instead by focusing on what you appreciate, love, or what makes you feel joyful. You can also simply get quiet and allow your natural state of well-being to bubble to the surface and bring your innate joy with it. You can shine this sun brighter and brighter.

You might think you will make others feel bad or worse if you're in joy when they're not. In actuality, you're demonstrating what it's like to exist beyond pain, beyond suffering, beyond dullness or boredom. You're inviting them into this higher, lighter, brighter experience based in Unity and Oneness. It will always be up to them to choose for themselves. You can't get sicker to make another better, yet you can bring the "All is Well" consciousness through and extend it to those around you, inviting them to also let the light in, the joy in, the ease back into their experience. You cannot control their choice, but you can be an inspiration, a signpost in regard to their well-being.

The Rollercoaster of Extremes

Imprinted by movies, television, and collective unconscious thought, the ego identity is societally programmed to gravitate toward extremes. So from that polarized perspective, joy might only be thought of as this overwhelmingly ecstatic, blissful experience. And while it can be experienced in this way, the true self knows and appreciates joy in even its most subtle forms. From your ego's lens, you might reach for overwhelmingly blissful Hallmark moments, and when you're not experiencing them, you swing to another extreme like depression, anger, or upset. Here, you'll bounce up and down like a rollercoaster, constantly seeking moments of overwhelming bliss, running toward fairy-tale endings, and being upset when you're not experiencing them. You then judge yourself and the more "negative" experiences as bad or wrong, which causes unnecessary suffering. You use excessive amounts of energy bouncing around like this, which could otherwise be used to create and align with a more unified world.

The ego's idea of bliss and happiness is different from that of the true self's perspective. The ego seeks fantastical outcomes and fairy-tale endings, and its happiness depends upon conditions, while the true self appreciates and en-joys the present moment without being attached to the details of what's happening. One brings temporary satisfaction and is based in lack and judgment. The other is a constant outpouring of sustainable joy because conditions are not needed to produce happiness.

What the ego might judge as boring or uneventful, because it's constantly seeking or opting into the extremes, the true self knows that even the most subtle energies based in joy are precious, natural, and good enough—*more than good enough*. When you grow tired and weary of the rollercoaster, you find that those moments of peace, those subtle sparkles of joy in your field, in your body, feel more valuable and obvious. You welcome these more subtle, refined experiences rather than needing extreme highs and lows or what you might have previously labeled as "exciting" or "entertaining" and believed to be a requirement for your happiness.

Instead, you recognize these things as unnecessary dramas, and you put those wild-goose chases to bed. You then wake up to the constant, even-keeled joy that has been inside you all along.

The soul does not *seek* joy (or anything, for that matter). It simply knows that it *is* joy. So allow joy to bubble up from within you. As you do this, joy begins to color your world in wondrous ways. The running around and seeking cease as you relax back into your innate, joyful nature.

The Expansions and Contractions of Ascension

As you awaken from the deep, sleepy trance of separation consciousness, new light-encoded frequencies will enter your being and expand your awareness.

This is a joyful experience, as you will feel lighter and brighter in your body, in your emotions, in your thoughts. As you continue to open your heart, you will experience yourself and the world through the lens of appreciation. You will feel more playful and curious about your life events and your true passions. In certain moments, you will feel like you are floating in the blissful clouds, above the drama and details that used to engulf you.

You will feel more deeply connected to others, even strangers, and you will want to engage with them in loving and uplifting ways. You will see their beauty and magnificence; you will look deeply into their eyes, and they will serve as the mirror for the unconditional love that you have cultivated within. This experience of expansion is a precious gift and a response to the inner work you have been doing. Yet it is important to note that each expansion is followed by an experience of contraction.

As these new energetic light frequencies flow into your beingness/body/field, they kick up the old dense patterns, emotional debris, and mental clutter that had previously weighed you down. When this gets kicked up or surfaces, you might wonder, *Why am I having this reoccurrence with an old pattern? I thought I was over this.* Or, *Why am I experiencing these heavy emotions just like I did years ago or as a child? I thought I was over that.* Yet the layers, the remnants or debris of that pattern, were buried deep within you. Nothing is wrong. What's actually happening is you're receiving the opportunity to clear away this dense baggage for good by allowing it to be witnessed and expressed fully in a space of deep allowance.

While contractions may not feel comfortable, they are a necessary part of your awakening process. When you welcome them with loving and open arms, embracing them as the alchemical gifts that they are, you allow the light of your soul to emerge from within. These dense energies that surface were the trapped emotions that those younger parts of you didn't originally know how to process. Whether formed from a childhood, past-life, or ancestral trauma, all you need to know is that now they need to surface, be expressed, and be relinquished. These dense energies are also the limiting beliefs you had created from the perception of separation consciousness. You can allow the light of your soul to shine loving awareness on these unconscious programs, beliefs, and emotions. The more presence you can bring to these experiences of contraction, the easier the density will flow through and out of you.

DANIELLE KORT

Allowing Yourself to Feel

Have you ever freaked out? Your mind starts running; maybe your breath gets short? You have no idea what to do, and you're not sure how everything will work out. All you know is that you're having a mini or full-on breakdown! And then you let yourself cry. Or scream. Or throw a tantrum. You go full out. You let it all out!

You expend that energy by letting it be expressed. You cry like a baby until you have no more energy. You feel empty. And then you realize that, in this moment, all is actually well. You're safe. You're okay.

The fears in your mind are more distant now, and you feel more clearheaded. Your breathing becomes more relaxed. You kind of feel like laughing. Or maybe your breakdown involved laughing and crying at the same time. The laughter feels lighter now.

You realize how dramatized everything felt before. But you've just moved that pressure-filled, exaggerated energy out of your body, and you feel better for it. Possibly much better! You might feel some gratitude for this new, clearer energy, or you might suddenly receive clarity about a next step. This soul guidance comes readily to the forefront, whereas before, the veils and overlays of fearful thoughts and dramatizations had covered up that guidance.

We can only feel joy to the depths that we allow ourselves to feel heavier emotions, like grief, anger, or heartache. This doesn't mean we need to wallow in our emotions but rather allow our feelings to express themselves as they surface. When purging dense emotional energy, we don't need to attach a story to the emotion because it doesn't matter where it came from, just that it needs an outlet. As we allow ourselves to become aware of these surfacing emotions, facing them, feeling them, and letting them move through our body and energetic field within a new space of awareness, we free them. We free ourselves. Afterward, we feel lighter, and new possibilities arise.

At the fundamental level, emotions are a band of frequencies that you tune in to. None are bad or wrong. You don't need to control or repress them. You don't need to dramatize them or indulge them. You can simply allow them to express as they arise.

If you have tears behind your eyes or pain in your heart and you are not prepared to feel the emotion to the depths of its presence, then you are in resistance. If you're afraid that feeling your difficult or painful emotions will cause you to manifest more of this, then that very fear is creating more pain for you. As intense as those emotions might be, if you can allow yourself to feel them deeply while also radiating compassionate awareness, you are expressing your multidimensional gifts. Even in the darkest of moments, emotionally or otherwise, if you exercise your faith muscle, you are assured to see desirable changes eventually take effect.

When we express our emotions, we cleanse and return to equilibrium. As we allow our emotions to flow freely, we eventually come out the other side. So let yourself cry, scream, feel discouraged. But then introduce the presence of the caring mother within you, and let her hold the inner child until there are no more tears left. You are the mother and the child, the uplifter and the one who is being uplifted.

Bring your full presence to every situation, every person, every experience. From this broader place of awareness, you have no need to judge "what is." Even if you're crying uncontrollably and have no idea why, or you're so furious you could punch your fist through a wall—it does not matter what the experience is. Simply be in the experience, be with the experience, observe the experience in neutrality—and eventually *be* the experience, remembering that you are one with it. Let the energy flow through you, knowing that all experience is happening for your highest and greatest growth.

Facing Your Pain

Unconsciously, we don masks or identities that seemingly protect us from the pain we collect throughout our life. We want to bury the pain or trauma so we don't have to face it. This pain feels so real, so threatening. How could we ever revisit that devastating moment from our past?

We spend a lot of energy, time, and focus avoiding this pain, which we created and clung to from an unconscious lens of perception—the painful stories we created, the hurtful words of another we absorbed, the places inside of us where we didn't know how to forgive or let go. However, if we shove our pain away into a dark corner of our consciousness, we lower our frequency, restricting the flow of joy and life force energy.

When you learn to face the pain, you can deal with it at the root. You can heal it, transform it, and expand beyond it, freeing up a lot of energy, which you can then put toward what your heart is calling you to express, experience, and create. We do not have to go digging for the pain that has been buried for years or even lifetimes. But if it gets triggered by a present-day incident or if a destructive pattern unearths the trauma which originated it, then it is our duty and honor to sit with that pain inside compassionate awareness and feel it to the depth of its presence.

The reflections in your life or dream will show you which pain needs your attention at any given time. It's not always easy to look at it, but as you take ownership of it, you can see it for what it truly is: a figment of your intoxicating imagination showing up in your dream as real. That's how powerful we are as creators. We can manifest our own personal hell just as we can manifest our own personal heaven. When we resist the pain or fight against it, we make it more real, and we rearrange our life again and again in order to avoid it. What we're really doing is avoiding feeling emotions that simply want to be felt, acknowledged, and faced head-on.

To deny or suppress inner pain, many people distract themselves with addictive behaviors, numbing what they don't want to feel. These addictions might show up as drinking alcohol or caffeine compulsively, smoking, binge-eating, or gossiping excessively—running toward things that divert you from addressing your pain. Yet as you try to escape, you are running from something that wants to be witnessed, felt, heard, seen, experienced. What you are running from are parts of you that need your presence. As the observer, you can bring your loving awareness to meet the emotions and parts of you that you had previously shoved down.

Rather than trying to stuff yourself full of distractions, habits, and addictive patterns, you can know that emptiness serves a purpose. That purpose is being able to fully feel yourself and bear witness to what needs your attention. This empty space is where your true essence has room to emerge.

Our protective ego identities employ defensive strategies to protect us from our pain, but this keeps us running forever in fear. The traumatized parts of us play out destructive behavior until we cultivate enough self-love and awareness to make a shift. As we choose to shine light on these parts of us through self-observation and presence, eventually, these ego identities dissolve.

You will have moments when you feel completely empty inside as this loss of identity creates more space within you. To the ego, this is scary and threatening because holding on to identity equates to its very survival. Yet the emptiness allows for more light quotients to come in and new possibilities to emerge. The emptiness may feel uncomfortable at first, but just know that it means more space is being made for love.

In this empty space, you may be in the question mark of what you want for your life. You may forget details about your past. You may not feel a sense of passion or enthusiasm, but perhaps a sense of neutrality and nothingness instead. This does not mean you will never feel passion or direction for your life again. Nor does it mean that in moments when sharing your past experiences could support another, that these memories will be inaccessible to you. It simply means that you are being reset so that you can align with your Higher Self perspective even more. So welcome these experiences of emptiness, knowing that it is not apathy or hopelessness but spaciousness expanding you. This space of nothingness helps to clear the dramatizations, extremities, and chaos formed by the ego.

Pain is a teacher; it shows us where we've been limiting ourselves and stopping ourselves from expressing as divine, powerful creators. It shows us where we have separated ourselves from the wholeness of what we truly are, from other beings, and from nature. It shows us where we have ventured off into fear and gripped onto fleeting feelings and trivial thoughts. Yet it's only a matter of time before the illusions fall away because they were always meant to fall away as you merge back into your truth.

We can grip onto the pain of separation through to the end of a lifetime or across lifetimes, but eventually, your truth will be known. You will come back to pure presence and the safety inside your heart, inside your core. So why not give yourself a break and let go of the pain now? You can face it, acknowledge it, honor it for what it has shown you, and let it move through and out of you for good.

The Power of a Lighthearted Outlook

As we grow into adulthood, play is often put on the back burner. In fact, some adults believe play is only for children. Yet dressing up, being silly, playing make believe—these are such innate parts of who we truly are. Becoming overly serious hardens us into cynicism and negativity. It dims our joyful inner light.

As we relax into a more playful attitude, life becomes more like a fun game than a mathematical equation that we must get right or be doomed to hell. Our attitude shapes and creates our experience, and as we lead our lives with a lighthearted deposition, we bob to the surface of a more joyful existence. If you've ever watched children or even cats play, you'll see how their curiosity leads them on fun and magical adventures. If we, too, can see other people, ourselves, and our world through the lens of curiosity rather than judgment, accusation, or condemnation, we can melt the rigidity that blocks our joyful expression.

Laughter is another catalyst for raising our vibration and opening our hearts to enjoyment. Laughing is the secret ingredient to a happy, more love-filled life. It brings people together and engenders belonging and unity. Laughter lifts our spirits and helps us put aside the melodramas and problems, which improves our health on all levels. Being able to laugh at ourselves, even in the midst of a challenging situation, helps us lighten up and feel more hopeful, optimistic, and empowered. We come alive when we laugh, and this keeps us in the moment rather than being anxious about the future or depressed about the past. We were born with the gift of laughter, and when we use humor to unify and uplift rather than divide or belittle, we bring ourselves into greater harmony as a collective.

Blossoming into Passion

When you are touched by the beauty of a painting or the fragrant smell of a flower, you feel it inside. It's a visceral compilation of your joyful soul's expression. You do not have to understand *why* it makes you feel that way, although your mind might try to put words to it. But this feeling surrounds you and enlivens you when you allow it to. When something enlivens you, sparks your interest, and tantalizes your taste buds, it opens your receptors. When you are open to this exploration of sensory and extra-sensory perception, this sets you on a path to fuller experiences, and more joyous moments emerge.

We tend to lose that sense of aliveness when we work in a passionless job, come home and plop on the couch, watch mindless television or endlessly scroll through social media until we fall asleep, then get up and do the very same thing the next day. This mechanical approach numbs us and detaches us from life. We feel dead inside, and we lose that sense of excitement, adventure, and passionate joy that comes from spontaneity and immersing ourselves in what truly lights us up.

Finding inspiration can be a great first step in connecting with your passion again. Rather than staring at a television, go out in your backyard and dance in the rain! Travel to and explore a new place. Jam to your favorite music. Go out in nature and admire its beauty. Inspiration can be found everywhere; you just have to be open to receiving it.

Making it a practice to tune in to what opens you, excites you, and impassions you helps you align to what is true for you. When you feel your heart blossoming open, lean into it, go with it, and see where it leads you. Your truth is synonymous with your soul's joyous expression. Only you know what is joyous and expansive for you.

You might be tempted to weigh your fiery passions against the rules or obligations of the outside world. But there is no need because your joyous passion is the only compass that you need. It is your North Star, the lighthouse beacon that guides your way. If only you will release the judgments and mistrust about your unique life's path. Your joy can light up a room, a stadium, the entire world. So relinquish your need to compare or question what you feel within and trust that what is emerging, which feels so good, so true, so delicious inside of you, *is the way.*

CHAPTER 8—WILD IN WONDERMENT

There is this universal force of energy that feels wild in essence. But it only feels wild to the conditioned, domesticated mind, to the mind that says this is the way you *should* behave. This is how you are *supposed* to live your life and dream your dream. These boxes that we put ourselves in restrict this flow of energy. Yet this energy is ready to burst forth from within you at any moment.

Your wildness feels scary to the ego. It might feel a little unfamiliar, and yet it is completely innate within you. Like a lion acting on its instinct, knowing intuitively where to find its next meal, knowing the right moment to pounce, we, too, have this instinct, and this instinct leads us through our life's beautiful unfolding.

Following our instinct can be irresistibly adventurous. The true self finds adventure fun and exciting, uplifting and inspiring. It is only to the conditioned, domesticated mind that the adventure feels scary, threatening, or something not to be trusted. Yet when you act on what you perceive as your wildness, your innate instinct, you begin to remember how trustworthy it actually is. Each step you take in sync with your wild nature guides you to these higher, lighter, and brighter experiences. You start to claim the rewards for listening to and going with that flow, and it begins to feel natural … because it *is* natural for you. Your work then becomes uninstalling those societal programs which kept you from your truth.

Each step you take with your wild nature feels so good, so aligned, so true. Each of those moments in flow, in sync with your true self, the Universe/God/Source, feels like *this* is what you were born to do, born to be. You're not meant to push forward toward perfection (or the ego's idea of perfection) based on other people's opinions, expectations, or rules. Nor are you meant to resist or stagnate, stopping yourself from being in this flow due to fear or distrust.

The domesticated human believes he must formulate blueprints and checklists for a successful life using his logical, linear mind. Yet these manufactured plans lack the sheer magic and divine synchronicity that come from following your heart. If you try to follow another person's roadmap, it may serve you for a while, but eventually, you'll find yourself at dead ends, disappointed, exhausted, and constrained, as if your wings have been clipped and your unique, authentic voice squashed. This is because you were not born to be an imitator. You were born as an original creator and always will be.

You have a customized divine blueprint within you, curated specifically for you, personalized to meet your soul's highest evolution and most brilliantly unique expression. Your Spirit holds this divine blueprint within your energetic field, within the Akashic Records. When you line up with your unique energetic flow, your unique energetic signature, and that energy begins to radiate from within you, everything starts clicking into place. This is what we call synchronicity. You find yourself in the right place at the right time, meeting the person you "needed" to meet, who seemingly magically appears at the perfect moment.

In the grand picture, everything we need is *always* within us and around us. Even when we're acting from the ego's agendas, we're always lining up with what we need in order to learn and grow. Yet when you move to the receptive, surrendered state, surrendered to your inner guidance, you can more easily *see* the synchronicities unfolding before you, and with greater ease and speed than you can when you're working in the denser, more restrictive states of consciousness—the calculated, willful ways and fear-based strategies of the ego.

Going with the Flow

Picture yourself flowing down a river. From your restless ego mind perspective, you're never going to get to where you want to go because there are tree branches and boulders you must maneuver around. It's seemingly treacherous and not a smooth ride. You might even be trying to paddle up the river, unknowingly, not understanding that you're making your journey much harder for yourself. But when you're working in flow *with* Spirit, it's as if you're going down this river, and the path is clear, smooth, more ease-filled. It's the most joyous and exhilarating ride. Your Spirit feels wild and free rather than captive to a treacherous and less-than-enjoyable journey.

When you begin to listen to your inner guidance, it may feel like the call of the wild. Surrendering to this wild abandon might feel scary at first. These "risks" you're asked to take may not seem reasonable or conventional —they probably aren't. This guidance is curated specifically for you, for your individual soul's path. You were not born to emulate other people's lives, but to live and stand in your truth and express your soul's unique gifts. If you look to the outside for other people's opinions about your specific path, you're just asking to get lost in the weeds.

Your truth lies within *you*. And only you. If you're looking for crystal clear guidance, you must go within. This is where the clear waters flow. This is where your joy and fulfillment bubble up from within you; the guidance that points to it and the feeling and experience itself are all within you. The old, outside world ways will not teach you how to answer the call of the wild. They will train you into obedience, where you will feel the need to turn around and attempt to control others and your life's conditions. Only in that deep surrender to your true self can you honor the call of the wild and flow with the ease, enjoyment, freedom, and fulfillment that you so crave.

What Truly Matters

It can become an unconscious habit to get caught up in trivial matters of the mind, but these tiny matters do not matter to our free spirit. They only inhibit our wild essence from flowing through us. Thoughts like, why hasn't he called yet? He must not like me. Or, he said, she said, it must mean this or that. We get so caught up in our mind running through possible dramas or scenarios that have nothing to do with our soul's desires. Like a runaway train, we abandon ourselves and this present moment, yet this present moment is all there truly is.

Our domesticated mind has been groomed to glorify movie stars and idols, status symbols, and impossible standards of beauty. But … what if none of this truly mattered: the name brand of your car or clothing, your job title, your appearance, the number in your bank account? In school, you're given a rating: a high grade means you're a good student, a low grade means you're a poor student. Whether stated or not, the indications are clear.

In society, if you have a big house, you are thought of as rich or successful, and you are considered better than someone with fewer physical possessions. The one without a house, possessions, or "accomplishments" is deemed unworthy, unlovable, untouchable. We can deny individuals and groups of people just as we can deny or repress parts of ourselves. However, this denial cuts us off from our wholeness. Every person is worthy of love, regardless of what they have or have not done.

In truth, it is all love at the core. It is only our mind that makes judgments of right or wrong, good or bad; that separates us from them, you from me; that finds reasons to war against or hide from the other. These fear-based perspectives are only an illusion, and it is time to put them to bed as you gradually awaken from your nightmare of separation.

You did not come here to emulate another's idea of what it means to live a full life. You came here to explore the human experience and practice opening your mind and heart, even in the face of challenging circumstances. You came here knowing you would have endless choices and opportunities to fulfill your soul's quest and experience your heart's deepest desires. You knew your choices would not be judged universally as right or wrong, and the word "failed" would not be stamped upon your forehead if you ventured away from your soul's perspective.

You knew this was going to be an exploratory adventure, a creative and enlivening journey. You knew your choices would help you discover your true wants and desires and you would learn through the process. You could see that your life or dream is more like a painting than a mathematical equation. If you paint something you do not prefer, you can simply paint over it with a different color or texture, and it's an ongoing expression of your divine and creative nature.

The Body Talks

Your body has an intelligence of its own. When you move and flow with your body, it is natural, delicious even. When you stop yourself from moving freely, you resist that flow of energy wanting to move through you. We might stop ourselves due to fear of what others could think or what we're told is appropriate or not appropriate. These limitations we place upon ourselves block our innately beautiful expression. So tuning in to your body, feeling into what it needs in any given moment, like what will nourish it, will set you on a path toward greater expression. Is your body craving movement or exercise? Is it in need of specific nutrients? Does it want physical touch?

As you give your body permission to communicate with you, you might find your jaw wanting to open widely or unfamiliar sounds wanting to express from your vocal cords. You may find yourself naturally toning or making "mmm" sounds in moments when self-nurturing or self-soothing is needed. You may find your body wanting to stretch in ways it has never been stretched before. This is your innate intelligence doing its part to help you move out of dense energies and expand into your light body. You can trust this innate intelligence, even if it seems weird to your logical mind.

When you are in flow with the natural rhythms of the body, with your wild and free essence, you are more in tune with what your body needs. At any moment, you can directly ask your body what it needs, then tune in and listen. When we learn to honor our body as the temple that houses our soul, our body is more equipped to provide us with our over-arching need: optimal well-being. When we feel good in our physical body, it is easier to feel good in our emotional and mental bodies. When we deny our body of what it needs, like sunlight, nutrients, rest, water, movement, and physical touch, we restrict that flow of life force energy, our muscles tighten, and our system struggles to support itself. We feel stagnant or stuck, restricted in our ability to comprehend what's going on, foggy in our mental capacities. When we give our body what it needs, it becomes the platform for our greater awakening.

When you see someone lit up about life, their eyes sparkle as they speak, their words flow smoothly from their vocal cords, their creations are awe-inspiring and brilliant. These people have something in common: they feel good in their bodies, and they allow Spirit to flow freely through their being. Your body is an expression of the divine nature that you truly are, and when you treat it this way, it expresses this way. How you relate to your body determines not only how you feel about yourself but also how you show up in the world. When you treat it poorly, you limit your divine expression; you cut yourself off from that stream of well-being. When you treat it well, that wellspring of well-being is overflowing, and you open a portal to unlimited amounts of energy. You no longer need things like caffeine to fuel you because your body has all it needs to sustain and maintain itself.

Be Easy on Yourself

As you move with your true self, as your true self, you exist in a space of timelessness. There is no rush here, just as there is no boredom. There is no expectation of being anything other than simply the full-blown expression of your divine nature. What if you were to let yourself off the hook? Free yourself from the harsh expectations of your ego? There is unlimited freedom here; freedom to simply *be*.

Remove the checklists, the obligations, the expectations for even just a moment and feel the peace that breathes through you, as you. You are good enough, worthy enough. It is not a question here. If tears come up as you read this, As you rest into the ease of this beautiful moment, allow them to flow. Surrender the struggle and simply relax.

This sensation may feel different or unfamiliar from what you have known, but *this* is your wild and wonderful Spirit blossoming forth. This new space of consciousness is yours to play in. We often forget how to play when we are wrapped up in the conditions and expectations of the mind, but play is such a natural expression of our soul!

When we feel space inside of our heart, we are like innocent children again. We don't feel silly playing hide and seek or naive engaging with others in light-hearted ways. We simply remember that this is how we are meant to feel in our day-to-day activities. We can play with life when we stop taking life so seriously, when we stop judging the unfoldment of our journey.

When you can remember to laugh, especially in those moments that have toppled you over sideways, and you can lie on the ground, and instead of beating yourself up, you look up at the stars and simply view life from a different perspective, out of curiosity rather than condemnation, then you can move through anything life hands you. In this surrendered state, you can simply smile and know that your dream is a wondrous and wild expression of exactly what you need.

You might believe you need to be "perfect" or to look or feel a certain way that's acceptable to others, but inauthentic for you. This only keeps you gripping in fear and control. As you remove the pressures you have placed upon yourself, you automatically align with your most genuine expression. Here, you dance with life, not to perform but to express yourself in ecstasy and with lighthearted ease.

Finding Resolve in Your Choices

There might be moments when you feel lost, as the wild path you're treading looks so very different from the one you see others walking. This is when you stop comparing your path to anyone else and remember that it is *meant* to look and feel different, entirely unique, in fact, as it is customized just for you! If another person questions your choices, go within and ask yourself, Is this person's perspective true for me? Then determine for yourself what feels resonate or nonresonant with your soul.

Find resolve for why you are choosing what you're choosing, expressing what you're expressing, and if it is out of alignment, make that shift back to alignment. Continue to dedicate yourself to this alignment with your soul. When you are resolved from within yourself, the reflections before you will demonstrate this. You will no longer experience other people questioning you or judging you. Instead, you will see that all before you syncs up with what you now believe about yourself. Stay true to yourself, stay true to your path, and know that this is the most profound way to honor your life and what you are here to embody.

The whisperings of your Spirit will only grow louder and clearer as you walk your path of sacred sovereignty. Self-doubt will melt as you grow stronger in your ability to be in this receptive state, surrendered to your heart's calling, as you heed that inspired guidance. Here, all unfolds more miraculously, more smoothly, and more in alignment with what you truly desire to create and express.

Take time for yourself every day to *feel* your true expression, to *feel* your connection to All That Is, to exist in the peace and serenity of your higher heart. Here is where the knots, the limitations, the traumas that you stored inside yourself can be worked out, like a deep tissue massage from Spirit, from the

Universe, from Source Creator Consciousness. Surrender to this loving gift and let your burdens go. You do not need to figure it all out yourself. Just simply relax, allow, and know that you are deeply loved and honored just for existing.

The Deep, Wild Woods

When we become so affixed to our daily routines, we don't give space for divine surprises that would like to reveal themselves. The ego identity likes "safe" and "comfortable," yet this can block our wild and free spirit from expressing. You may want to know what's going to happen next every single time, and you can try to control your experience, but this need is coming from fear. By surrendering to the unknown, trusting your Spirit to guide you, you allow for a fuller, more joyful life experience. Rather than waiting for the other shoe to drop, which is a fear-based perspective, you can open your heart and learn to trust your inner guidance.

Imagine taking a walk through the woods. If your ego is leading you, you might peer around every corner, anxious about the possibility of being attacked by a big animal, fearing that you may get lost and never find your way. Or you might just want to turn around and avoid the journey altogether. But if you can tune in to your Spirit, your wild essence, that innate navigation system within you will guide you along a beautiful and exciting path.

Prudence is different than fear. In exercising prudence, you may see bear tracks and decide to go a different route. This doesn't mean you're in fear; it simply means you are using discernment. Your instinctual nature is grounded in infinite wisdom, so you can trust that in going off the beaten path and allowing yourself to get "lost," you will always find your way. Wandering or getting lost actually helps you discover your true self, your true essence. It is in those moments that shake up your status quo and challenge your tightly held beliefs or previous understandings of your world that great transformation can occur.

Your true self, your wild essence, cannot emerge if you are holding on so tightly to what you believe you have been or who you believe you are. Removing yourself from the monotonous circles you have been running in allows you to free yourself. Getting off that hamster wheel of the ego identity, gaining distance from the programs that have been running you, breaks that old energy. It allows you to see through fresh new eyes. When you are in unfamiliar territory, this causes you to create new neural pathways, new connections to how you interpret your experience.

You are never truly lost, but you can disconnect from your truth. This disconnection is actually more acute when you are so attached to your to-do lists, routines, and obligations. Concrete jungles might seem more civilized and predictable, but this heavy cement barricades you from your inner knowing, from your satellite connection to Spirit. When you follow your Spirit through the living, breathing woods, through the unknown, that connection becomes stronger and stronger. As you follow your heart, your navigation is clear.

Rewilding Yourself Back to Life

Rewilding is coming back to your soul's true expression, as the soul is wild and free in nature. Your untamed essence is one in which the programs of a conditioned mind no longer impress upon you, and you exist purely in a state of conscious awareness. It's where your journeys through unconsciousness feel like distant lands that no longer support who and what you now remember yourself to be. You now express yourself with wild exuberance and a fiery passion that lights you up from the inside out.

In the past, you were motivated by external forces, conditioned beliefs about how you "should" behave or how you "should" live your life. Here, you are free of those expectations, those limiting ways, which served a purpose for your third-dimensional experience but are no longer applicable to this state of pure presence where you now reside. Here, you sing and dance and play with wild abandon, abandoning only those restrictions you had once placed upon yourself. Here, you are light-hearted with your words, easy-going with your actions. Here, you surrender to your heart's true callings. You are humble and nimble in your choices, and your dream reflects this. Long gone are the days you felt bound to anything that you are not.

Your wild, free nature carries you like wind beneath your wings as you soar to greater heights than you've ever known. You are quick-witted, nevermore doubting the words coming out of your mouth or the expression being birthed by you. You do not burden yourself with how others perceive your expression to be. You simply close your eyes and allow your body to move as it wishes. You feel free to express yourself passionately and fully. Not a care in the world could stop you from moving with your Spirit as your soul's truth.

You have set down the baggage of the domesticated mind and are acting in accordance with a higher power. You have surrendered the will of the ego, or the small self, and exchanged it for something much greater. In doing this, you have broken the chains that had bound you. You have emerged from the dark cave where you had been hiding in separation.

You walk out into the flowery fields where Unity and Oneness wrap you in a warm blanket of unconditional love. You find yourself skipping through these fields where love and inclusiveness abound. Here, you are safe. You have come home. You walk with curiosity and appreciation of this lighter, brighter experience, which engulfs you and welcomes you to express yourself creatively, boundlessly.

There is no judgment here. Here, you want what's best for all beings, and the reflections of your world demonstrate this. You lie down next to a flower patch, and you look up at the sky in wonderment, thanking all of Creation for its artistry, for dancing with you and around you. You are not concerned with how you look or whether what you say or do is the "right" thing. You are simply existing in love. And nothing can interrupt your deep connection with nature, with your true, eternal nature.

As you embody this beautiful expression of the Divine, you are not focused on what is going to happen next; you are not regretting what happened before. Instead, you are deeply enamored with this present moment. As you commune with the beauty all around you, you feel so safe and supported that you want to jump with joy and cry with laughter. You are too focused on the wonderment all around you to let small, little details bother you right now.

There is a river nearby, and it calls to you. The wild current beckons you toward it. You dip your toe into the cool, cleansing waters, and you're inspired to strip away your clothes. You jump into the waters and immerse yourself fully. As you emerge, your naked, unencumbered body feels cleansed, healed and purified. The minerals have soaked into every cell of your being. You feel enlivened with energy, with vitality. You dance with the current, making your way down this river, allowing its wild yet gentle flow to guide your way. You realize you are one with the river and that nothing can stop you from moving blissfully along your path of wild freedom.

CHAPTER 9—SACRED SOVEREIGNTY

Our expansive Spirit has a vast imagination, which goes far beyond the ego identity's musings. The out-picturing of your dream, of your life experience, becomes confining when all you can imagine is what you've seen before. You can replay the same scenarios and habitual ways you've become accustomed to, but you are designed and destined to create far beyond this. Negativity, trapped emotional traumas, submission to rigid rules, and expectations created from fear are what keep you cycling through old, unconscious realities. When you free yourself of these limitations, you reclaim your sacred sovereignty.

Sovereignty is the freedom to be and express all that you truly are, regardless of past experiences, cultural norms, ancestral patterns, or other people's expectations of you. When you raise your vibration to match that of your wild and free spirit, you surpass the restrictions that once bound you to a world of fear and separation. There are countless ways to realign with your sovereign expression. One is to stay true to your deepest expression of self. Staying true to yourself requires you to trust yourself. And to trust yourself, you must know yourself.

We become intimate with our true expression by getting honest and real with ourselves. Where have you been lying to yourself and others? Where have you pretended something was fine when deep down you felt angry or agitated? Where do you put on a mask and try to perform and conform to meet the expectations of others or your own ego identities? Looking at these places with love and compassion can assist you in shaking off whatever has been holding you captive.

We are not free when we come from fear. Sovereignty is about moving in sync with our boundless Spirit and letting go of the fears in our minds. Being a sovereign nation means creating regulatory structures that best suit that nation's unique wants and needs, regardless of what neighboring nations are choosing for their body politic. Being a sovereign soul means creating your world on your terms, regardless of what you've been told is acceptable, plausible, or normal.

Taking Your Power Back

When you are autonomous, you know what your boundaries are. You know that what *feels* right *is* right for you. You allow your natural instincts to guide each of your choices. You do not live to please others or act in ways that are incongruent with your inner knowing. You are not bound to rules, regulations, or systems that go against your truth. You simply disallow these things from having a hold on you by releasing your hold on them, by disengaging from *them*.

You get to create your world. This is your absolute birthright. In school, you are taught to follow the rules and not step out of line. Yet as you awaken, you will begin to realize that many of these lines are restrictive to your expansive Spirit. These rules or expectations serve you while they do, but as you remember what and who you truly are, you will feel the urge to move beyond them.

If you feel a glass ceiling above you or a tight box around you, this is your invitation to recognize these limitations and expand beyond them. We cannot do this if we give our authority away to false authorities outside ourselves. If you believe talking heads in the media, teachers or gurus, religious leaders or bosses have a greater say in shaping and creating your life than you do, then you are giving your power away. Your creative say becomes diminished. Your creative powers are dependent upon the permission you give yourself to live your life on your terms.

It is rather silly to believe that you are powerless and at the effect of another's dictates. Sometimes we use others as an excuse not to follow our heart, but this is just a funny game we play with ourselves. No one can stop you from fulfilling your destiny unless you allow them.

Let's Get Really Honest

We reclaim our sacred sovereignty by choosing our highest truth moment-by-moment, by choosing to stay true to ourselves over our ego's fears or agendas.

It can feel uncomfortable or scary to choose anew, but that discomfort, fear, or suffering comes only from the ego perspective. The more you get comfortable with getting uncomfortable, the easier it becomes to access the light of your soul and then integrate this higher consciousness into your physical, emotional, and mental bodies. As you do this, you broaden your perspective, making it easier to see those limiting patterns and old ways that no longer serve you. We let go of those patterns and habits by observing them and no longer engaging in them. We expand more and more as we do this.

An example of this might be an old pattern of people-pleasing. Although it might feel more familiar or comfortable to please someone rather than being honest, you can now feel that taking that old familiar action is not in alignment with your greater truth or your inner knowing. As you align instead with what your True/Higher Self is asking of you, you further integrate your truth and allow the old unconscious patterns to fall away. You do not engage in those old realities or dynamics that are no longer aligned with who and what you know yourself to be. A new reality emerges because of this.

This new reality is the lighter, brighter, more expansive reflection of your higher wisdom. This is what it is to exercise your sacred sovereignty, to be sovereign in your truth. You can feel the difference between acting out of old, unconscious patterns and acting courageously from the inspired guidance within you.

Your truth might look different from another person's truth, and you don't need to shame or blame yourself or others for having different perspectives. You can simply give yourself permission to act on your inner wisdom. This requires knowing your boundaries and recognizing what your personal sacred yes or sacred no is in any given situation. You do not need to influence or control another person's version of their sacred truth. As you align with your soul's truth, you set an inspirational example of what it looks and feels like to be congruent with the universal flow of All That Is. Trust that others can and will be inspired by your demonstration of this.

Exercising Your Free Will

We can exercise our free will to make choices that most contribute to our greatest well-being, but sometimes we forget that we have this freedom. The ego identities we create, the attachments we form to outer world constructs, and the belief systems created from fear, lack, and limitation restrict our ability to be in our sovereignty. Have you ever been in a situation where someone demanded something of you, and while it may have seemed like a requirement, it didn't feel good in your body or like it was the best choice for you? But because this person was so insistent, and perhaps it made logical sense, you went ahead and did it anyway.

Later, did you notice the consequences of your choice? You might have thought there was no choice in the moment, but we always have a choice, as mandates cannot be imposed upon us unless we allow it. That feeling in your body was your inner guidance system. Maybe that choice could be true or highest aligned for another person, but that doesn't mean it was for *you*.

Even when situations feel difficult or cause conflict, it is imperative that we listen to and follow our own truth or inner guidance. Throughout your life, you are exposed to all kinds of messaging, beliefs, and "shoulds" about the world. You can lose yourself in others' opinions about what they believe is right or wrong, good or bad, true or untrue. Yet when it comes down to it, what really matters is that you discover *your* inner truths, that you uncover and reunite with your true essence. You can begin this process by discerning between what feels resonate or in alignment for you versus what you've been told, taught, or modeled from outside of you that does not align with your beliefs or values.

The Power of Taking Space

To really know yourself, you disentangle from whatever has separated you from the truth of your being. Often, this requires you to take time or space away from society or those relationships where you have been deeply rooted in old dynamics or beliefs that no longer serve you. These relationships might be with childhood friends, family members, or people who don't support your spiritual growth. This time or space doesn't mean that you will never see these people again, but it will allow you to recalibrate with your divine energy, with your higher or more expanded expression. Once you have come back to center and you have become more grounded in your own sovereignty, you can reevaluate whether or not these relationships are in resonance with your new energy. It is important not to attach ourselves to any particular person or relationship, as this could stunt our spiritual growth.

We do not need to burn bridges or walk away from relationships in a dramatized or harsh manner. Instead, we can simply step back and retreat into ourselves for purposeful amounts of time. In doing this, any old codependencies or relationship dynamics that hold us back from experiencing and expanding into our greater truth can be worked out and relinquished. In order to know ourselves in this new light, it is important to create a safe environment where we can reflect on that which is no longer in alignment with what we are discovering ourselves to be.

This safety comes from within us, from our connection to God Source Consciousness. We do not find it by looking outside ourselves. It is by going within that we tune in to our soul's truth. The revelations about what you came here to embody then become crystal clear, and you are able to perceive coherently, in alignment with your heart's true callings. It is in your heart of hearts that all the answers you have ever been seeking reside.

We uncover our hidden gifts and talents by getting quiet and listening deeply to what is being communicated to us and through us. If we are too busy and distracted, trying to perform in the ways that are expected of us, we lose sight of what wants to be birthed from within us. Going off into the woods alone to commune with nature and your Higher Self does not make you crazy or woo-woo, as some might believe. It is a rite of passage into a higher understanding of yourself and your world. Giving yourself this time and space away from bright lights and city chatter, from well-meaning friends and family, is one of the most important actions you can take along your path of conscious evolution.

In sitting with yourself in quietude and reflection, you allow your inner knowing to emerge. When you know yourself, your true self, you are able to handle situations with grace and wisdom. You show up in love, as love, without getting pulled into dramatic interactions from a triggered, old identity. You come from a place of compassion rather than condemnation, and your loving awareness lifts you to new experiences that are gentle and kind.

Upholding Integrity inside of Compassion

As we mature into the sovereign beings that we truly are, there comes a point when our integrity becomes more important than the need to conform or fit in. Wanting to belong is a natural desire for a human being. So learning to flow within social constructs when they are in integrity with your soul and breaking tradition when they are not becomes an art form. Rebellion does not have to be violent, harsh, or judgmental. Simply opting out of belief systems, rules, or cultural expectations is really all that is required since your free will is inherent. We do not have to fight or look down on those with differing opinions or life choices. We can simply create our world by expanding our consciousness, focusing on that which ignites and enlightens our soul.

We do not participate in the co-creation of New Earth by going into combat with the old structures that are already outmoded and crumbling on their own accord. We co-create and participate in the design of New Earth by honoring our sovereign truth and supporting the new structures, which are built upon a foundation of respect, honor, and love for all beings. If an individual is attempting to control other beings, they are simply acting from their own limited and fear-based perceptions. We do not assist these individuals in rising to higher consciousness, where love is ready to meet them, by condemning or crucifying them. While we exercise our sovereign boundaries and hold others to their highest levels of integrity, we also cultivate deep compassion and understanding for their position in life. This is what frees us and simultaneously frees all others.

Throwing mounds of guilt and shame upon another doesn't mean they will become aware of their unconscious actions. In fact, the absence of love and compassion is often why these individuals continue to play out their unconscious patterns. They act out in the first place because they were never shown this grace. If we can remember that we, too, have acted from unconscious spaces and places within us, it becomes easier to open our hearts and be the reflection of love they are so unfamiliar with. We, too, would want this in those moments when we act out our unconscious patterns.

Being in our sovereignty does not mean we close our hearts to those who do not resonate with our new, expanded states of awareness. It means that we drop our egoic needs to save or fix those who are making choices that don't align with our beliefs. If another comes to you asking for support or advice, feel into the situation, and if it is in alignment, be of service in a space of nonjudgment and compassion. You do not have to go knocking on doors in an evangelistic manner. This only creates resentment in those you are chasing after. When you share your truth with the intention of expressing your soul and being an uplifter, rather than trying to convert another to a particular dogma or prove your ego's worth, you are doing a great service.

Your soul's truth is not the opinions or judgments of your ego's identity. Your truth consists of the new understandings that reveal themselves as you learn from your old, unconscious habits and patterns and you decipher between what you once thought you were and what you now understand yourself to be. This will continue to change and evolve as you shed your old skins and your soul's expression emerges.

Your truth is best expressed through the inherent gifts you were born to enjoy and share with others. These gifts often get buried underneath limiting beliefs and survival-based priorities. They emerge, however, as you open your heart to the truth of your divine essence. There's a multitude of ways to express your God-given talents. Examples could include the arts, such as painting, music, or energy healing; humanitarian efforts, such as providing food and shelter to those who are in need; creating new education systems that better support our children's ever-evolving needs; leading or way-showing by sharing your wisdom; or spearheading sustainable initiatives for alternative or renewable energy.

What's important is that it flows from your heart and expresses from pure intent. Standing on a soapbox so you can be right about something and trying to show others that they are wrong is an act of ego. Yet showing up in love, as love, with a message of hope and upliftment, truly caring to understand where others are coming from and what they're dealing with, is the courageous action of your Spirit.

Your World Is Your Domain

Sovereignty is a choice; it's a choice to be your own being, to dance to the beat of your own drum, to relinquish the need to reach outside of yourself for anything. When you are rooted in your sovereignty, you know that all the answers are within you, and all you have to do is ask, get quiet, become present, and pay attention. Sovereignty is not about "going it alone," it is about learning to trust yourself while remembering that you are immensely supported and guided along your spiritual journey. It's about radiating your true, authentic expression, shining your light, and sharing your gifts, even if it makes other people's ego identities uncomfortable. It is about being courageous and stepping into your truth moment-by-moment.

When you stop reacting to everything "out there" and instead cultivate deep presence, deep awareness inside, you reclaim your inner power and create your world from the inside out. Your world is your domain, not from an egoic perspective, but from a birthright you were given upon agreeing to this incarnation. How would you like your world to be? How would it look idealistically?

You do not have to wait for others to make a move. In essence, you cannot. It is going within—transforming your own density, shadows, and limiting perceptions—that creates and aligns you to this world you wish to participate in. Your world is your creation, and if you would like to create it on your own terms, then you must give yourself the space and nourishment to allow your soul's truth to emerge.

Your ability to be with yourself in silence radically enhances your capacity to embody your true sovereign nature. When the chatter of your busy mind falls to the wayside, your soul's voice has space to emerge. It is in these quiet moments that you can more easily observe what is no longer true for you as an individual. It is in removing yourself from things like herd mentalities or social constructs born of fear that you can know the higher, more expansive universal truths, which are based in love. We give ourselves, *gift* ourselves, this spaciousness so we can merge back into Unity Consciousness.

In letting go of old dynamics, systems, and versions of people, we free ourselves to open to new versions of these systems and people if they are still in resonance with the greater truths we expand into. Otherwise, we become a vibrational match to new ways, systems, and people altogether. Again, it is of the utmost importance that we not attach ourselves to anything or anyone out of fear of the unknown or the new that would like to greet us in a more loving and welcoming space of consciousness. It is in your highest and best interest to continue expanding into an unconditionally loving and kind-hearted world. You do not need to see the ending of friendships or relationships as "loss," as it is really just a new chapter for you, one where the people in your outer world reflect back to you your new heightened senses of awareness. When you radiate love, honor, integrity, kindness, and respect, this is what you will receive in return.

Whatever is not a vibrational match to your new frequency will be rearranged and transformed by the infinite intelligence of your universe. It is futile to attempt to control or fix anyone's behavior that is displeasing to you. If you feel you're being disrespected, for instance, simply go within and see where you lack respect for yourself or where you don't feel worthy of being respected. Your outer reflections will always show you where there is opportunity for greater alignment. It will also show you what is working in your favor. You can expand on these beneficial creations and learn to let go of the rest.

To reclaim our sovereignty, we resign from trying to control our outer world reflections. Sovereignty comes when we forgo the need for others to behave how we think they *should* behave, and we let go of needing things to be a very specific or particular way. We take our power back by taking responsibility for our creations, observing and responding rather than reacting to them. When you look in a mirror and see yourself frowning, you don't try to change the *reflection* in that mirror, do you? You simply smile and watch the reflection change before your eyes.

Life responds to your energy. It can be no other way, as it is divine law within this universe. Remember, your thoughts, emotions, words, and actions create your outer life experiences. You have the power to be at cause rather than at the effect of what's happening in your world, but only by creating from the inside out.

You are more powerful than you may know, and with great power comes great responsibility. When you respond to life, rather than reacting from fear, your response-ability grows. Responsibility is not a chore but a rite of passage into your higher expression. Every sovereign being revels in the glory of their *ability* to remain present, observe their outer world reflections, and *respond* with loving awareness.

The Fall of Social Dominance and Hierarchy

Many generations have learned to focus on what separates them from the whole, not by celebrating what makes them unique but by criticizing and fearing their differences. They see their neighbors and their choices as a threat, fixated on differences in skin color, religious preference, and philosophical approach, and they judge what they cannot understand. They condemn and attack those they believe are going about things the "wrong way."

They buy into old beliefs that categorize people into classes or caste systems, and they position themselves as better than or worse than another based on social standing, economic status, or appearance. These beliefs can be quite unconscious until you put a magnifying glass on them and discover that they are in fact there. Placing yourself or another on a pedestal is a belief created from separation consciousness. It disallows your heart from connecting with others in the pure and innocent ways it is designed to.

A beggar on the street is no better or worse than a trader on Wall Street. In the eyes of God Source Consciousness, we are all innocent children doing our very best with the ways we have learned to perceive. We can be sovereign in our choices while still remaining true to our heart's inner knowing that we are cut from the same cloth as our dear brothers and sisters. There are different phases to our awakening process, and in stepping back, away from the cultural tendencies we had learned to imitate, prioritizing our soul's inner journey, we can come back around and reintegrate physically with others. By untangling from old belief systems and dynamics that no longer reflect our soul's truth, we can then re-engage from a more expansive and unified perspective.

Social dominance and hierarchy are things born of a fear- and separation-based illusion. So tuning in to our heart's inner knowing and radiating our inner power, which includes our freedom to choose sovereignty, is all that is really required to remove ourselves from these illusions. We can be sovereign in our choices simply by following our inner guidance and aligning with our soul's truth on a moment-by-moment basis. Sovereignty is something we were born with but forgot as we were hypnotized by outer world distractions and into controlling systems and structures. We must remember, however, that we agreed to play this game, to move through these illusions, and to free ourselves by waking up to our unconscious realities.

No one outside of you has any more power over you than you allow. You are a sovereign being in a freewill universe, and it is within your domain to focus upon, agree to, and engage with only that which empowers you and enlivens you. This is what a conscious creator does, is, remembers herself to be.

DANIELLE KORT

Sacred Individuality

Our individuality is meant to be honored and celebrated. If we all created in the very same way, we would encounter a stagnancy, which would be extremely limiting to our creative nature. To evolve into a unified consciousness does not mean you have to think, feel, and experience exactly as your dear brothers and sisters do. You incarnated into the physical plane with the intention of playing with perspectives and expressing your uniqueness through your creative endeavors. The freedoms you have to choose your own adventure are insurmountable. The uniqueness you have expressed up until this very moment pales in comparison to the degree of sovereignty you were given at birth. It is time you allow your creative expression to color your world in wondrous ways, as you are one of a kind, and the world is ready to hear your soul's song.

Sovereignty is your divine birthright. You are never stuck with your circumstances, and your choices are never sparse. Energy is constantly moving and shaping in response to that which you are radiating vibrationally, energetically. Your presence is sacred, and it is your right to align with your truth. What is true for you as an individual expression?

Along your path, you will face circumstances and situations that ask you again and again, What is your highest truth in this moment? Your highest truth is that which aligns with your Higher Self, the future version of you who's calling you forward. We can become infatuated with what others think, believe, or have drawn conclusions about. We can become enamored with what we see on social media, on television or in movies. But these ideas and beliefs are only perspectives, perspectives among millions and millions; lenses to see through, ways to live a life among millions and millions.

As children, we learn to pick up on the cues of our parental figures, teachers, and those who we give authority to. This serves a purpose for as long as it needs to. Yet as an awakening being, you are gifted the opportunity to choose anew—to see through a fresh lens and expand your awareness. Stepping outside of old, restrictive vantage points and expanding into these new possibilities allows your soul to express itself more freely.

That larger part of you knows that you are an unlimited creator and are not bound to restrictive laws or rules based in fear, greed, or control agendas. These are only fearful perceptions of a conditioned mind. As you awaken to these restrictions that you have placed upon yourself and you open to these new worlds of possibility, you start to trust yourself more, and your intuition begins to lead the way. This lights your path more and more. You realize you no longer have to agree with others' ideas or beliefs that don't align with who and what you truly are in this now moment. You realize that no one is forcing or controlling you to be or do what is nonresonant for you.

So go ahead and open the old, dusty shutters which once kept the light from streaming in. Allow your Inner Spirit to light your way. Choose to stay true to yourself, even if it means forging a new path, one that looks completely different from the others around you. There is a wild freedom that comes from forging this path, from entering this new frontier of consciousness. Your Spirit will guide you to new experiences that enliven you, that allow you to take on these fresh perspectives. If only you will go with the flow of this higher guidance.

The Heart of a Lion

We stop ourselves from experiencing the new, expanded awareness and realities that emerge from higher consciousness by "should-ing" on ourselves, by comparing ourselves, by playing within the bounds of what is socially acceptable or expected of us, simply for the sake of conforming. This is no longer a requirement of us and never truly was. Yet our fears have kept us bound to these denser realities, which were born of control, suppression, and restriction. We can choose to shut down our soul's expression out of a need to conform, fit in, or appease others' expectations, but when we muffle our Spirit, we dim our light. We dam up the life force energy that wants to flow through us and be expressed by us. We place ourselves in restrictive boxes. And the flame of our unique, fiery passions grows somber.

Here, our life feels dull and contrived. We feel like sheep following a captive herd, one to which we don't feel like we belong but feel indebted, like indentured servants. Picture your soul as the lion who forges her own path. The one who goes off on her own to find herself in the wild and, after months, if not years, finally returns to her pride for deep connection, camaraderie, and sharing. She is the one who knows herself as an individual expression of the Divine, who thinks and feels for herself, and still knows how to work in collaboration for the betterment of her pride (or soul tribe).

Be the lion who knows herself beyond herd mentality, beyond what she is told she is or should be. Forge your own path, draw your own conclusions, and always hold these conclusions lightly, as they are bound to shift and change as you transform from within, as you align back to your True/Higher Self perspective.

There will almost surely be a period where you feel lonely, like a lone wolf, as you go off and discover yourself from the inside out. However, know that there is great purpose in this transitional time where the old, limited ways and perceptions begin falling away completely. This time is meant for you to retreat into yourself so you may lay new foundations for your experience, which are aligned with your soul's truth.

As you align with these new perspectives and open to these new worlds of possibility, other like-minded and like-hearted souls will come into your experience and relate to you in new ways that are in alignment with who you now know yourself to be. You will eventually find a community (come-unity) soul tribe. Trust your True/Higher Self to lead you to embody your sacred sovereignty. In pulling away from what once entangled and bound you to limiting ways, you will free yourself to return to deeper connections and relationships in coherence with your purified heart. Allow this process to unfold in perfect, divine right timing with grace and gratitude. Allow the beauty, wonder, and awe of your life's unfoldment to engulf you in an ever-present experience of Oneness and Unity as you gradually awaken from the sleepy slumber of separation consciousness.

As a beautiful expression of the Divine, you were born with the ability to choose at will. This inheritance holds great value when you understand which choices bring you greater freedom and which choices hinder your creative freedoms. When we give our authority away to false authorities outside of us, we muddy our connection to our true source of power, which is God Source Consciousness. It is the inner child who wants what she wants but does not know the difference between want and need. We can allow younger parts of ourselves, our ego, or others to direct our will until we finally realize that our creativity is stunted and that soul fulfillment can never be enjoyed by going in this direction. As we surrender our will to Divine Will, our freedoms and powers to create become infinite.

CHAPTER 10—SOUL EMBODIMENT

The process of embodying your soul is much like the process of a caterpillar becoming a butterfly. In the beginning stages of this spectacular transformation, a caterpillar's natural instincts tell it that it's time to prepare its cocoon. Inside the cocoon, the caterpillar's body begins to break down and eventually turns into a gooey substance. The caterpillar trusts that this is a natural part of its evolution. It allows the old to be transformed into the new as its cellar body is restructured and reformed into something quite beautiful.

It waits for that moment when this time of incubation is coming to a close. As it emerges from the cocoon, it is delighted to find that it has a completely new body and magnificent wings, which will carry it into the next chapter of its life. You, too, are growing wings as you emerge into your light body, as you express as your beautiful soul. So allowing this process to transform you from the inside out is to assist in the undertaking of this momentous journey.

We are fully guided through this process of transformation, and this guidance comes from our Higher Self. As you remove the distractions and reactions of your ego identities and you tune in to presence, you are led on a treasure hunt of recollection. In recalling your true, divine expression, soul embodiment naturally takes place. When you get out of your way and make space for this natural process, you introduce an ease and effortlessness into your experience. We make it harder on ourselves when we try to force spiritual growth from the will of our ego, when we try to figure this all out with our logical mind, when we run from the changes we are guided to make, or when we believe we need to see the whole picture before taking that next step on our path.

If a caterpillar, who has only ever known itself to be this earthbound wormlike creature, doubted its evolutionary process and natural instincts, if it resisted its extraordinary, transformational unfoldment, it would have a difficult time becoming the butterfly it was destined to become. A caterpillar may not be able to imagine itself as a butterfly, but that doesn't stop it from surrendering to the organic expression that wants to be birthed through it. Rather than worrying about how it will ultimately make this transition, the caterpillar does what it instinctively knows to do moment by moment, and with each step along this evolutionary journey, the creature blossoms into all that it was meant to embody. You are in a process of transforming your world from one of fear to love, of density to light. You are evolving from a caterpillar to a butterfly. This journey is not for the faint of heart; it is for the courageous heart. It is a courageous thing to move into the unknown and embody more of what you truly are.

Attuning to Your Higher Self

While you might know intellectually that you are Spirit having a human experience, it is something else entirely to embody this knowing, to embody your soul. One is a concept that can be fleeting or fickle, the other is a welling up of energy, which becomes a fully realized experience. Embodiment is allowing our soul or Higher Self to "take the wheel" and surrendering what we once thought we were.

For awhile, who you believe you are has to do with what you identify with "out there" in your physical world, such as your physical attributes or body, the number in your bank account, your job position, your marital status, the political party you've joined, or your nationality. You can be in physical form knowing that these things are part of the human experience, yet it is the ego that clings to, attaches to, and defends these identities, because who are you if you are not these things? At some point, we become ready to know ourselves on a deeper level, and we access this knowing through presence, by being one with this eternal now. It is also through presence, and only this way, that we can recognize our restrictive ego identities. In presence, we can practice self-observation, and this is precisely how these ego identities dissolve.

In this embodiment process, you are becoming one with your Higher Self. The relationship you have with this "future" you, or more expansive you, is the most impactful relationship you will ever form. Meeting your soul or Higher Self with deep reverence, respect, honesty, trust, integrity, and love is how you come to embody your soul once again. Your Higher Self exists in higher dimensional spaces of consciousness. Yet it is not just one self but can be many different higher selves who guide you at any given time. They are all you in these higher octaves, as you are all selves, all beings, all things simultaneously, but have just fallen outside of this remembrance.

At first, you are channeling your Higher Self as you tune your channel into that higher vibrational frequency. As you tune in, sense (see, feel, taste, smell, hear) or perceive your soul's messages, and move with inspired action, you come into greater alignment or vibrational harmony with your soul. This is because in doing this, you are honoring your Higher Self or soul and this honor engenders intimacy and synergy. Forming this relationship is not only about listening, but also about speaking to your Higher Self. You do this in a peaceful, surrendered state by directing your focus to your higher heart, which is where your Higher Self resides. It is within you. Speak silently or aloud to communicate that which you desire to express.

Speak to your Higher Self as if he, she or it were your best friend. Share your needs and concerns, request assistance, ask for guidance, and state your sincere intentions. Then pay attention to all the ways your Higher Self may respond. As you learn to vibrationally tune yourself moment by moment, moving into and remaining in those higher states of coherence, eventually you allow your soul to be fully housed within you.

For a certain amount of "time," only part of your soul is able to stream into your experience. Your soul is made of light and is not a vibrational match to the density of the physical, carbon-based body. So in uplifting your vibration and your consciousness, you activate an alchemical process and prepare a space for the entirety of your soul to be housed. This space, or inner dwelling, is called the light body. Your light body is an energy body or a "suit" that you wear in these higher realms of consciousness. Once your light body is fully activated, you are enabled to move at will between dimensions, realities, and worlds.

As your physical, mental, and emotional bodies of consciousness purge the density of the lower realms, your energy body or light body activates. For your light body to fully come online, each of these bodies of consciousness described above rises in frequency to merge and unify with the light of your soul, and they begin working together as one. Everything inside of you restructures and realigns to harmonize in a higher octave. Here, you become merged with the One Unified Consciousness, and your Higher Self now becomes the captain of your experience.

DANIELLE KORT

Exiting the Fear Matrix

When we formed protective ego identities on top of our soul essence, it was because we were adapting to live in a world we had found to be fearful, a world not to be trusted. These identities acted as coping mechanisms, which protected us for as long as they needed to. In those times when we were less aware, they served a great purpose. We can thank our ego identities for caring enough to keep us safe. Yet as we evolve into our expansive soul expression, we no longer need the protection that we once thought we did. The reflections in your life's dream will continue to unfold naturally and show you what you have been holding on to within and have been weighing you down. In each of these moments, you can choose to continue crawling in this world of fear or grow wings and fly above it.

When you wake up in the dream you are experiencing as reality, you will clearly see that the nightmares you were having were manifestations of your innermost fears, insecurities, and inner conflicts. To engage in the distorted perceptions of the small mind is to continue replaying old records that have nothing to do with who and what you truly are. Give yourself permission to remove your hand from the turntable, to take your foot off the gas pedal, and step away from the illusions that have told you that you must be fearful of the world around you.

When you move your consciousness into a state of fear, you link into a fear matrix. This fear breeds more fear and creates dissonant experiences. As you return to love, you tune in to grids of light and harmony, and joyful experiences become your new normal. Bring your awareness back to that beating heart of the universe, that eternal pulsing, that breath of life, which is never separate from you but that you have simply disconnected from at times. Allow *this* to be the foundation from which you grow. Embody your true essence in this space of pure potentiality, pure peace, pure joy; where nothing needs to be different, better, or fixed; where well-being simply abounds. Imagine what the reflections of your experience would feel like, look like, if this were the space you were tuning in to and existing from in each moment.

How Unconscious Creations Materialize

In the unconscious realms, we knew not what we were doing. We can liken this to someone who sits day in and day out with their head hunched over a technological device, like a phone or computer. This person begins having symptoms such as headaches and a stiff neck. So he reaches for something to cure the pain; perhaps something like aspirin or liquor for a numbing effect. But the pain is only being covered up, band-aided for temporary amounts of time, and the pain persists.

One day, this person realizes that perhaps this pain is being caused by his posture. So he begins sitting up straight, and blood flows easily to his brain again. His headaches go away, and his neck is free of pain and constriction. He got to the root of the issue.

At one time, you acted in unconscious ways, and these unconscious ways caused pain and suffering. You likely reached for an endless number of things outside of you to relieve this pain. Little did you realize that your unconscious beliefs, emotions, habits, and patterns were the very source of this pain. As you take the time to reflect on your thoughts, emotional reactions, and choices, you can get to the root of your pain. As you shine your loving awareness upon it, with compassion and empathy, you free yourself of it. You can then make new, more conscious choices, and your world is transformed from one of pain and suffering to one of joy and exaltation.

Your soul exists in full presence, in conscious awareness, as conscious awareness. Your ego identity was indoctrinated with separation-based meaning-making. We grow spacious as we set down the painful perspectives and stories that we created and clung to from an unconscious lens of perception. Our conscious awareness grows as we take responsibility for where we have caused ourselves pain and disharmony. When we realize that we are the ones we've been waiting for, we can stop waiting for someone or something outside of us to "cure" us, and we can begin to *participate* in this momentous process of transformation.

Awakening to Unconscious Patterns

Becoming aware of beliefs, patterns, programs, or even realities that no longer serve a purpose for your ascension into Unity Consciousness and then letting these go will become your new mission as an awakening being of light. Again, if we choose to ignore or resist the changes we know we need to make or if we cannot see clearly that something needs to shift, eventually our Higher Self will step in to make these changes on our behalf. Remember, it is not loss, rejection, or bad luck. We have not done anything wrong or bad. Realities, situations, or people are removed from our life when they start to impede our soul's evolution here. Everything is happening *for* us as we live in a benevolent universe; it is only through a blurry lens of fear that would have us see otherwise. Like a loving parent who truly knows best, your Higher Self assists in making space for your heart's deepest desires to manifest by removing that which anchors you to denser realities.

If you see that you have placed yourself between a rock and a hard place, you can begin the negotiation process between your Higher Self and your smaller self. While your smaller self may feel stuck in this space, your Higher Self sees it as an opportunity to upgrade in consciousness. If you can see the rock and the hard place as an opportunity to review your circumstances in a new light, get uncomfortable, and choose anew, then you can free yourself again and again. You are a powerful creator with unlimited ideas to express and create that which your soul desires to be and experience. So remember to trust that whatever is unfolding before you is an opportunity to refine and co-create the life of your dreams, to dream that big dream of your Spirit.

Being in the world as your soul's true expression, you embody this as self. You forgo the need to continue interacting in the old, unconscious ways, and instead, you take a step back and learn to let them go. The Higher Self does not judge the old patterns or ways of doing or being. As your Higher Self, as your soul expression, you simply observe the unconscious patterns with neutrality. You say, "Oh, I didn't realize I was doing that until now," and you simply let the pattern float by, no longer engaging in that way. Embodiment is not an instantaneous occurrence but a gradual succession of soul-aligned choices.

The Reunion of Your Soul Aspects

As you honor and embody your soul, your abilities to co-create grow. Your consciousness is an extraordinary force, but when this force is going in all directions, your abilities become diminished. When parts of you are fragmented or separated—whether it be body parts, organs, or tissues that are experiencing a state of separation, whether it be your inner child, past life versions of you, the parallel reality versions of you—your intentions become muddied because there are many things going on all at once. As we unify these aspects, these versions of us, we become more powerful in this creational process. Our intentions and energies align and flow in one harmonious direction as we return to a state of coherence.

When self-care goes out the window, this is an obvious sign that a part or parts of you are in resistance to your greatest growth and well-being. In this instance, you can ask that part of you what it needs. Perhaps it needs rest, an afternoon of creativity or play, or maybe it just needs a moment of acknowledgment. We unite our soul aspects by honoring them, shining the light of compassion on them, and giving them the love they didn't know how to give themselves. We cannot create powerfully when we come from a place of resistance inside, so it's imperative that we honor each of our inner aspects within a space of loving grace. Like a shepherd, we herd our soul aspects back into the unified field, uplifting them with the divine frequency of love as they make themselves known. Together, we return to a unified state of consciousness.

When you do not accept certain outcomes or situations in your life's dream, then you are not accepting those *versions* of yourself that have experienced or could potentially experience those situations. As you return to living and loving unconditionally, you envelop all the aspects of you in your warm, loving embrace. This does not mean you forgo your sovereign right to move toward realities that light your soul on fire. It simply means you are unattached from needing the outcome to be a certain way. You accept what your universe has in store for you because, with every situation, there is gold to be mined. It is a "both/and," a surrender and an action, a beautiful, sacred dance.

When we surrender and let go of our resistance to past, current, and potential outcomes or experiences we do not prefer, we no longer unconsciously draw them to us to be experienced in the physical realm. We have love and compassion for those versions of us that would otherwise experience them, just as we have love and compassion for other people who may experience those situations. In loosening our grip of resistance on unwanted experiences, we free ourselves of the judgment we have placed upon those situations, aspects of us, or other people who might experience them.

If we would like to move into Unity Consciousness, then anything we have identified, labeled, or defined ourselves as must be met with unconditional love and acceptance. Any potential version of us, whether it be the "prostitute," the "homeless person," or the "mentally unstable one," is equally awaiting this same divine frequency of love and acceptance. When we can provide this, each of these aspects is reunited back into Oneness and Unity, identities and labels fall away, and what remains is our soul essence. Our judgment is what separated us, and our love is what soothes and mends our "broken hearts."

Turning Up Your Radiance

A naturally desirable magnetism occurs in the process of soul embodiment. When your heart is wide open and you are seeing through the lens of compassion, you naturally attract more loving people into your life. Your radiance makes you a bright light, and you light the way for others like a lighthouse beacon illuminating a dark and stormy sea. You are not tuned in to the dark and stormy realities anymore, yet you are spacious enough, bright enough, to be an inspiration for others' transformation.

By radiating your soul, you magnetize all that you truly desire to be, express, and create in your world. You do not compromise your true wants and desires, so now they naturally occur through you on your behalf. You have released the resistance and the inner conflicts. You have dissolved the density that had once gotten in your way of manifesting the dream of your Spirit. As you come into integrity with your Higher Self, your energies become attuned to the creation of All That Is. As you step out of judgment and into unconditional love, as you bless your circumstances and all those involved, you free yourself from a hellish experience of life. You wake up from the nightmare that had once felt so real.

When we merge with our soul, we are in effortless flow with the rhythms of the universe. We feel free to express ourselves joyfully and boundlessly. We honor ourselves and all life forms. We communicate openly and honestly with full transparency as we know there is nothing to hide. We are in integrity with ourselves and others as we have *integrated* each of our inner aspects back into their unified expression. We sing the praises of this beautiful miracle that we call life.

Flowing with High Frequencies

As you open to higher vibrational frequencies, you will have moments when everything just feels different in the best possible ways. Perhaps you notice how others are responding to you in this higher octave, with a bigger smile on their face than usual, as they lean in closer to fully take in what you're saying. Perhaps you seem to have a greater capacity to listen deeply and be a space of divine love as another vulnerably shares their current struggles with you. Maybe you feel more animated or lit up about a subject than you normally do, and the inspiration moves you to create something remarkable. These expansive experiences are meant to show you what it feels like to embody your Higher Self. It can feel freeing and exhilarating, and it can also feel a little unfamiliar. When you reach these higher frequencies, it is your opportunity to go with the flow of this new energy. You are invited to ride this wave, allowing your Higher Self to move through you freely and fluidly. Here, it is easier to access loving thoughts and feelings of empowerment, joy, and connection.

Taking up the opportunity to practice being in this new vibration assists you in beginning to reside here full time, and gradually you expand further and further into these higher states of being. Gradually, you become a closer and more concise frequency match to that of your soul essence. Even at this more expansive place of vibrational frequency, you will be tested with crossroads at every turn. Will you choose to flow with your Spirit, with life-affirming, good-feeling, unconditionally loving thoughts, communication, and actions? Or will you dip back down into old habitual patterns or automatic choices? Either way, you will learn from the experience. Yet as you become more proficient at working with your energy, you realize that moving *with* these higher, lighter, and brighter feeling vibrations provides you the freedom, ease, and fulfillment that you have always been seeking.

Again, with every expansion comes a contraction of sorts. Here, you can meet the old, dense vibrational sequences that are surfacing with the greater degrees of love and inspiration you had just been experiencing in your more expansive states of being. Little by little, you gain the agency to expand your consciousness with every in-breath and out-breath of this expansion and contraction process and you embody your soul expression more and more.

Unraveling the Construct of Time

Our soul exists beyond the construct of time. It remains merged with the One Unified Consciousness and sees no distinction between past or future, timelines or lifetimes. Our soul is limitless and boundless, perceiving only infinite possibility and never-ending choice. Time is a creation that separates us from the present moment. When we are too caught up running toward a "future" that we hope will be better than "what is" or fearing what will happen next, when we are too busy regretting our "past" or wishing things were the way they had been before, we are abandoning the present moment.

The truth of "what is" in this precious, present moment is all there truly is. Come to a place of pure peace inside yourself, knowing that what has been and what will be are divinely orchestrated and the precise medicine for your soul's journey here. Returning to this peaceful inner knowing helps alleviate and transform the fears, anxieties, regrets, and sorrows that had once bound you to a linear timeline. When you can find resolve in your "past" interactions and nullify your needs to strive toward a "future," you can return to the simplicity of this present moment and the ease and joy that accompanies it.

The *exchanges* within your past and future are all that truly matter. It is only when we cling to the stories that our ego identities create, the meaning we have made based on these exchanges or experiences, that we attach ourselves to a linear timeline. If we can surrender the stories, the meaning-making, and accept all parts of us, all experiences with compassion, then we return fully to this present moment. This exploration of the soul is meant to be a joyous adventure. It only becomes painful when the overlays of judgment cloud our perception. When we remove judgment, we see clearly. When we open our hearts, we return to presence.

The ego identity exists in boxes, adhering to linear timelines. The soul or Higher Self moves about freely without restriction. The ego identity is quick to judge and criticize while the soul holds all in unconditional love and compassion. The ego identity needs conditions to be a certain way, but the Higher Self lives and loves unconditionally. Our soul is at peace with how things have gone, with how things are unfolding, and continually guides us to make choices that will unify all as one. The ego identity is lost in separation-based thinking and is scattered in all sorts of times and places other than the present moment. The soul is purely at peace, existing right here, right now, in all moments. Our soul is ready to advance further into the forefront of our conscious awareness, of our experience, and as we open our hearts and tune in, we can commune with and embody our soul once again.

Living fully in the present moment means that often we don't know what will happen next. We are tasked with tuning in to our feeling, our intuition, which guides our way in every moment. What feels true for us can change on a dime as we change frequency more frequently. Acting on your soul's truth moment-by-moment is what you learn to do in order to *feel* your way forward.

Singing Your Soul's Song

As you awaken, you will feel the urge to express your soul in numerous ways. Soul expression comes in many forms. In the unconscious realities, we often discount our soul's expression. Singing joyfully in the shower might be thought of as silly or meaningless. Dancing to your favorite song might seem like a waste of time. Yet these are only your thoughts when you live in a world of fear and judgment.

When you repress your soul's expression, you stifle your life force energy, making it difficult for you to thrive or even be motivated to live. So to live fully, or to live at all, you *must* express your soul—passionately and unapologetically. It is here that you dance with deep purpose in your heart. If you judge your soul's expression as meaningless and adhere to only that which your ego believes it *should* be doing, you lose touch with all that you are here to embody.

It is worthwhile to inspire and uplift, to allow joy to color your world, to sing your soul's song. There is purpose in following the trail of your highest excitement and passions. It is not a far-off fantasy but a calling from within. Your expansive soul holds the blueprint for what this looks and feels like. It is only in feeling into it and moving with it that it shall be revealed to you, embodying it as divine inspiration emerges.

Any act of creation has a feeling behind it. Does it feel freeing, uplifting, bigger than the little you? Or does it feel obligatory, restrictive, or survival-based? The latter does not contain enough fuel to sustain you. Moving with this energy will feel like drudgery, and you will face dead ends again and again. So feel into what enlivens you now, even if it doesn't make sense to your logical mind. Allow your curiosity to be a roadmap pointing the way toward your soul's preferred direction.

DANIELLE KORT

Your Capacity to Serve

From the perspective of a conditioned ego identity, we were just trying to keep our head above the waters of survival consciousness because we thought we had to "go it alone." We were so busy seeking things outside ourselves because we thought these things would reunite us with our wholeness and bring us the fulfillment we so craved. As awakening beings, we come to realize that fulfillment comes from embodying our wholeness *from within* and radiating this unified consciousness to all other beings through the vibrational web that links us. In separation consciousness, we didn't have the capacity to hold this space of loving grace for other beings in our lives. We couldn't even do this for ourselves. Yet as we embody our Higher Consciousness, we can reach out and be in service to the greater whole. As we move in the direction of our inspirations and passions, we naturally align with those who will benefit from our God-given gifts.

Choose to take small, inspired action steps that will align you with discovering and sharing your unique soul's gifts and abilities. Choose to give yourself enough time and space to allow this inspiration to emerge. Soul embodiment is not only about "doing," it is also about "being." Sometimes you must be in the question mark about what you are here to share and express. While it may be uncomfortable, know that the space you are creating by surrendering your need to continually act is opening the portal for higher inspiration. An inspired life is contained in this precious moment, and all you must do is surrender to what wants to inspire you, what wants to be birthed by you, through you, as you.

Our greater expression is a multidimensional collection of Higher Self aspects that welcome our reunion with them. As we expand our living light to exist in higher states of being, eventually we come to embody All That Is. To find ourselves here, we love and accept all parts of us, all beings, and all of creation, because rejection only creates more separation. As you recognize that all parts of you have been beneficial for your evolutionary journey, you return to the perspective of your soul.

The butterfly does not emerge from its chrysalis until its transformation is complete, nor does it resist the urge to emerge when the time has come to soar to greater heights than ever before. When we try to push ahead or resist our hunger to grow, we cause ourselves suffering. When we exert great effort to get ahead of the game and then judge ourselves for not being further along, we suffer. When we hide from the changes we are guided to make, when we play it safe, when we compromise our inner knowing again and again, we suffer. As we move beyond social norms and beyond our ego's fears and expectations, we find our own rhythm, and we flow with what naturally wants to occur through us.

So let this evolutionary process transform you from inside out as you let go of the old, embrace the new, shine your light, and uphold that higher frequency. Allow your soul to have a voice. Give it the space to be honored, to be recognized, to be felt. Eventually, your radiance will illuminate your world in ways you cannot imagine.

CHAPTER 11—CONSCIOUS CREATION

Life is meant to be a celebratory dance, one where your joyous heart leads the way. You are meant to sing and laugh and play with passion and enthusiasm from the very start of your day. You are birthing and being birthed with every breath as you are an ever-unfolding expansion of All That Is. Why would you judge yourself or this miracle that we call life? Birthing does come with contractions, yet those contractions lovingly push us to expand, and your expansion is your soul's greatest desire. With this expansion comes greater possibilities, ones that you could not previously imagine; ones that are so beautiful, so extraordinary, beyond words, beyond definition.

Creation is your God-given birthright. To consciously create is to live in the fullness of all that you are. When we create from our soul, as our soul, we are fulfilled. We are at peace, and we dance with joy. Bringing awareness to what enlivens you tunes you into this most lustrous and loving energy. This energy molds and shapes your experience, decorating your path with the most profound and magical moments.

If something is making you feel stuck or stagnant, deadened or depleted, know that it may not be worth your creative focus. It could be a dead end or an inorganic timeline that is meant to collapse. A higher, more sustainable road exists for you. The on-ramp to this elevated road presents itself when you open your heart. So doing things that open your heart brings forth more people, places, and experiences to love.

At your core, you are a powerful creator. When you remember how to trust and love yourself, the glory within you becomes manifest. You can create from love, trusting in the divine orchestration of your life's unfolding, or you can create from fear, resisting your experience and turning your energy body into a hard defensive shell. You can hide in the darkness of separation consciousness, fearing everyone you meet, or you can face every person, every experience, with acceptance and love. The energy behind your actions determines your creational outcomes and manifestations. None of your choices are right or wrong; they simply have energetic reverberations.

The Energy Behind Your Creations

Feel into your body, into your energy, before you take any particular action. The energy behind your actions aligns you to the reality that is a frequency match to that energy. If you are sending out an email, pay attention. Are you feeling rushed, triggered, anxious? If so, then this is the energy you are sharing with your recipient and the energy that shapes your experience. All the energy you radiate impacts the greater whole.

Now, if your recipient is vibrating in a surrendered state of grace and pure compassion for instance, your energy will bounce right off of them, as the purity of this frequency cannot be affected negatively. Yet, there will still be a consequence to you in some form. Let's say, however, that your recipient is having a rough day and feeling down on themselves. By engaging with your recipient while you're in this triggered state, not only will your dense energy impact them but it will also call to you the reality that matches that energy. You will see this in how they respond or where the conversation goes from here. Instead, try centering yourself in presence first and then send your email within the divine frequency of love. Here, you would be inviting them into this higher or lighter space of consciousness, and this just might make their day. Of course, it would be up to them to choose to meet you here or not.

Becoming present and acting with conscious intention aligns you with the harmonious flow of All That Is. If your intention is to speak to the heart of the one before you and connect with them through the vibration of love, the creational outcome of this interaction will look and feel much different than if you are holding resentment toward them, for instance. Bringing your focus back to this precious present moment and relaxing into the purity of your higher heart gives you the space to be more intentional with your energy and actions. The more you practice working with your energy and choosing consciously, moment by moment, you build an energetic momentum that carries you into greater states of abundance, bliss, joy and all those things your soul desires for you to experience.

You can weave in the vibration of love with every breath, as every breath is a fresh moment, an opportunity to choose anew. You are never too old to make a new choice, nor are you ever too young. You are always ripe with possibility. So in this moment, if you were to do something you've always dreamt of doing, what would it be? How would it feel? Taking one step in that direction sets you on a path to a fuller, more enlivened experience of life. Then the trick is to keep going, as long as it feels aligned and true within you.

There is no need to force yourself to complete something if you have simply outgrown the desire or the experience. You can pivot to something that feels more inspiring and exciting in *this* now moment. This is what it is to be in flow with your Spirit and with life. You will continually expand into new and greater possibilities as you grow your consciousness. These are the creative freedoms you were born with.

It is within your domain to choose what lights you up, right here and right now. There are ways to weave together your passions so you can experience your multidimensional desires in concert. Use your creative imagination and capacities to their utmost potential and watch as your creations unfold with the most magical qualities—true to you, unique to you, and remarkably inspiring to others.

Live your passions for yourself, and allow their brilliant vibrations to touch the hearts of others. Your Higher Self knows that the energy you radiate while you live with passion and purpose is the transformational change agent the world needs most. So whether it is speaking or teaching, painting, singing, or creating in any capacity, what is most important is the energy *behind* your creations. Are you having fun? Are you enjoying the creational process? The outcome is only a piece; the journey is what truly matters.

Less Obligation, More Passionate Expression

One of the most important aspects of conscious creation is discovering your passions and your true calling(s), which are ultimately one and the same. When you know what your heart is calling you to create or experience and you act on it, you allow the innate joy that wants to burst forth from within you to be embodied by you. Have you ever been inspired by a fresh new idea and suddenly you began playing with the possibilities of bringing this idea to fruition?

Could you feel the joy and excitement present in every cell of your being? This is truly what we're here for and meant to experience every day of our lives.

It's easy to lose track of time and come into full presence when you immerse yourself in your joyful passions. You can feel love and passion in even the simplest things, like admiring a ladybug on your finger: being enamored with the beautiful markings on its shell, the way it makes its way across your hand, its teeny-tiny, little feet. You can appreciate the intricacies of life with a baby or with a pet.

You can feel passion through your creative capacities when you touch a pen to paper and watch the ink flow onto the canvas through your creative imagination and into your physical experience. The beauty in that, the deliciousness in *that*. You can revel in that. And this raises your vibrational frequency and expands your joy from the core of your being. It brings you soul satisfaction. It is a combination of witnessing in wonderment and creating in blissful bounty that opens your world to a sustainably passionate existence.

It's common, however, to take on and prioritize heavy obligations, duties, or checklists out of fear, like tending to the needs of everyone around you but yourself or being married to your job, leaving no time for those relationships that matter to you most. Society often dictates our drive or motivations, but when we allow these popular belief systems to rule our world, we lose touch with what's truly important to us. Common societal expectations might include getting married by a specific age, climbing the corporate ladder, or following the latest trend in fashion or health just because everyone else is doing it.

Pressures or expectations can weigh heavy on your heart. Your true self knows that they are simply unnecessary and not required for living a joyful and fulfilling life. These heavy obligations serve as blockages or resistance to our soul's full expression. Take inventory of where you hold these heavy expectations in your consciousness and then let yourself off the hook by removing these ego-driven priorities from your life. This will free you up in countless ways and create the space for your soul to emerge, where it can express itself in the boundless ways it is designed to.

When you come from a space of guilt or needing to please or fit in, you introduce more resistance into your actions. This resistance holds you back from flowing with your free and passionate spirit. When you relinquish these limitations and tune in to what excites you, what turns you on, you activate the immense powers of creation within. Following your inspiration is what aligns you to your highest creations. Whatever feels obligatory, heavy, or cumbersome in your experience is asking for some readjustment. There are certain responsibilities that may feel purposeful and aligned with your soul's calling that can be seen in a new light, perhaps by introducing more play and ease within these responsibilities. Then there are obligations or expectations that may seem logical but are not truly necessary as you walk your unique soul's path.

Opening Your Creative Channels

Have you ever had a dream of doing something really creative? Perhaps you want to write a screenplay, create a cookbook, invent a new household product, originate a different kind of art, or build your own business, but you find yourself putting it off because of fear, busyness, or other forms of resistance. When you act on your creativity, regardless of whether it makes you money or you even finish the project, you open a portal to higher consciousness because you realign yourself with the truth of your creative nature. Exercising your creativity enhances your creative abilities on all levels, including how masterfully you create your reality.

Creativity brings fulfillment. It nurtures the soul, nourishes the soul. Give yourself the space to allow creativity to blossom. Allow yourself to surrender and relax in a safe space; then creativity has a chance to flow through you. Your unique expression, brilliant and divine in nature, is meant to be shared. Just as with anything, though, there's no need to force or push it with an attitude like, *I've got to make this happen!* In doing so, you limit your creativity. You put boxes or restrictions around it.

Creativity is magic, or what we might call magic. Spontaneity brings this magic through and carries it forth. Creativity is seeded without control and blossoms with allowance, permission, and play. The magical child within you wants to come out and play. Yet so often, we unconsciously restrict ourselves with obligatory, shame-driven, guilt-ridden beliefs, and we stifle this magical, creative child's voice.

We get to create in magical realms, seemingly magical, because what we've known before was highly controlled, as we were trying to act in certain ways acceptable to society, to the groups that we belong to, to our family or co-workers. Feeling that we must perform or act in very specific and predictable ways squashes our creative expression. Acting in these socially expected ways might make you and others feel safe, but it dampens that spark within us: our wild and free spirit. Our spirit does not bow to false authorities or conform to rigid rules because these have nothing to do with what it knows itself to be. These are only limitations of the mind's programmed beliefs, ideas, and norms. Who's to say what's "normal" anyway? Who's to say what's "acceptable?"

No one has the authority to thrust their opinions or judgments upon another without their consent. Yet they can certainly try. They can certainly use tactics like guilting or shaming to discourage others from expressing themselves authentically, honestly, and freely. Yet as they try to control others, they control themselves at the same time. They limit themselves just the same when they continue to play in that realm of repression.

But *you* get to step outside of those boxes. *You* get to expand past those restrictions. *You* get to free yourself from the pain of suppression, from suppressing your free Spirit and your creative nature. No one can stop you unless you agree to the limitations you place upon yourself or allow another to place upon you. Allow others to choose what they choose, knowing that they, too, will awaken beyond their limitations.

Free yourself by listening to what wants to be birthed from within you. It might look different or odd. You might be labeled as crazy or woo-woo or out there. There are plenty of labels the domesticated mind may use to try to fit you and/or your creations into a box. Yet others' judgments are irrelevant. In a higher octave, your creative expression is sacred and honored universally, infinitely. Your creative courage is applauded and encouraged by many souls, even beyond this human collective.

You help yourself along your creative journey by getting to know and being guided by your true self. As you build your faith in embodying this, your creative expression unfolds naturally, organically. It blossoms forth without effort-ing or struggle or resistance. At some point, it just flows through you very naturally.

You can get this flow going by honoring the creativity that wants to burst forth from within you by taking pen to paper, paintbrush to canvas, by singing your soul's song. And not needing these creations to live up to any particular outcome; not forcing them into something that will make you money, buy you fame, or appease the endless ego fantasies. You can simply honor your creativity by expressing it with joy and passion and allowing the act of this creation to inevitably open new doors to exciting, fun possibilities, which will further expand this creative expression.

Eventually, yes, this can become your way of life. It can absolutely support you in the ways you wish for it to. But you must get out of your own way, out of your own head, to allow these creative channels to be an opening. You must loosen your grip on the survival-based beliefs, scarcity thinking, and fears about sharing your authentic expression.

Begin in a quiet corner by yourself, if that's what feels supportive to you, and let yourself go. See where your creativity takes you. Allow this new vibrational frequency, which has now been boosted by your passionate expression, to elevate your consciousness, to elevate your experiences, knowing that following your highest excitement is really the key to true fulfillment and a joyful life experience. You hold the key to your happiness. There's no need to hide that key from yourself just because you're afraid of what others will think or because you're afraid of coloring outside the lines or disobeying "the rules." These are only nightmarish fears that looped through your mind. You can set those down now and open the door to creating your new world based in freedom, freedom of creative expression, where there is no judgment, only blissful creation.

Materializing Soul Desires

Your true self plays with energies, with realities. You are here to express and create and move *with* the energies of creation. From this space, the resistant patterns of your mind no longer hold you back from flowing with life, with the dream of your Spirit, which you're here to experience and co-create. From this space, there are no heavy obligations, pressures, or monsters to fight against. There's only pure potentiality and the joy that comes from birthing those potentials to fruition. So from your magical child's perspective, what in your heart of hearts do you most want to play with, express, share with others within an environment of celebration and a true zest for life? Following your highest excitement is honoring your Spirit and paying homage to what you came here to embody.

You are the projector of your reality. What you see "out there" is a transmission of the frequency you hold within your consciousness. "Out there" is the physical version of what exists within you vibrationally. Your beliefs shape and create your reality, so whatever is alive, real, and tangible for you is what you believe. As you become more aware of your thoughts and beliefs, you can consciously choose which realities you prefer. You can use your creative imagination to visualize and see your reality the way you wish it to be. If you want something to materialize in physical form, start by going within, expanding what you believe, and opening your heart to the possibility of this dream emerging. Raising your vibration and playing with this possibility inside your imagination, using all of your senses to fully immerse yourself in this scene, brings you closer to the realization of this creation.

You are an extension, an expression of the Divine. There is no shame in your desires to create, to imagine, to dream. As you dream, simply notice where the ego might latch on to concepts and try to direct them in a way that fulfills its programmed agendas. Simply bring awareness to these places and let them go, cleansing these veils of illusion with your pure presence, coming back to this state of wild wonderment, knowing that you can align with whatever dreams or realities your heart desires to experience.

When we forgo the need to see what's before us or "what has been" as our only possibilities, we can open our imagination to new, extraordinary experiences. It is through our presence that all things become possible. When we resist what we do not prefer, we only draw these things to us more. When we accept what has been, what is, and what can or will be, we can transform our realities through the vibration of peace.

To consciously create is to create through present awareness in alignment with your Higher Self and its Divine Will. When there is something your heart desires to call forth into physical form, you can claim this reality through intention and through your deep desire for it to be so. When you receive the creative inspiration, the inspired guidance, you move with this energy to bring this desire to fruition. If any part of you is in resistance and fear when you visualize this desire, then you are blocking this desire from materializing. You must get ready, *feel* ready, for your new reality to emerge. Our Higher Self knows what is most dear to us, and as we raise our vibration, as we raise our consciousness and expect the very best of life to meet us, we automatically align with the realities that we truly desire.

Riding the Waves of Conscious Creation

Conscious creation is like learning to surf. You sit in the quiet waters of loving awareness, and when that collaborative wave is coming, you paddle to line up with it, not out of panic or trepidation or scramble, but in sync with the ocean. As that wave hits beneath you, sometimes you find your surfboard right in flow with that wave, and you ride that wave of conscious creation all the way to the shore. The exhilaration is palpable.

At other times, as you're learning this process, you might find that you miss the wave or that the wave crashes on top of you. And there is no shame in this. There can still be a rush of joy, of learning, of refinement. And there will always be another wave. You just notice where you were out of sync with the ocean.

Maybe you had tried to push ahead too aggressively, or you stalled on the opportunity to go for it out of fear. So what? That's okay. You're learning. And you can have fun while you learn. There's no need to take all of this so seriously. The joy of creation is what you're here for, so let it be a joyful journey.

The Collaborative Spirit

We are designed as creators, not imitators. When we try to produce from the ego or the domesticated mind, we might work to imitate or "play God." This is different than creating in connection with the Source we stem from and are one with. When we create from this connection, we are co-creating in *harmony* with All That Is.

When we try to produce from our programmed ego, we work *against* that connection. Sure, often in unconscious ways, we might not mean to, but we create more separation, more fragmentation. You might see this in military instruments of warfare or technologies that try to control or destroy other beings. These things are produced from a different intention and understanding of the universe, and there's much less power behind those creations.

When you work for and toward the greater good of all, the power behind you is inconceivable. You're working with the energy that creates worlds, and the aid and assistance that comes to your side is unreal. Yet it is so very real, so potent, because you work in collaboration with joy, expansion, and a love of life. You're not fighting *against* life; that's resistance. That's where you lose that true power. Here, you're like an ant trying to push a huge rock up a hill.

Instead, when you work in sync, when you play in sync, when you create in sync with the orchestra of All that Is, you're like an elephant pushing a pebble down a hill. It becomes easy, effortless even. You go with the stream rather than try to swim upstream. You work in flow; you're tuned in. And all that is really required is that you stay present and continue tuning in to that channel of higher intelligence, higher wisdom, higher love. Be the elephant, not the ant. Tune in; play with the orchestra, not against it. Surrender to the beauty of All That Is. There is no need to grip on tightly, trying to control everything or make things what your ego thinks they *should* be. Instead, relax back into this ever-present, ever-evolving flow of well-being.

The Power to Create

Many on the planet seek power. They feel powerless because they have forgotten their connection to All That Is. The breadth and depth of your power goes far beyond the human mind. It rests in your connection to Source and spills out from there. This power is a different kind than you make it out to be from the human perspective.

Power does not come from circumstances or conditions or things outside of you. True power is not about a job position, a government role, or the number in your bank account. True power is expressed through your presence. True power is not boastful or dishonest or tyrannical in nature. Those were illusions born of the ego.

True power is the ability to be with all beings in love, in compassion, in grace. It's the ability to remain calm and connected to your power source—that ever-flowing current of divine love. It's the ability to no longer judge those around you or the circumstances before you. It is an unwavering faith in God/Source/the Universe/Your Higher Self. It's the ability to no longer be deterred by doubt or fear.

True power resides in your choice to create from the limitless joy emanating from your Spirit. Your power grows as you allow your light to shine brighter, freeing your Spirit, opening your mind, and opening your heart to greater possibilities beyond what you've known and greater love beyond what you've experienced.

Power comes from trusting your inner guidance more than the physical circumstances before your eyes. It comes from dropping the resistance and allowing your flow, from being agile in each moment, from being moldable by your Spirit rather than rigidly fighting the transformation and creational force that wants to come through you for your highest and best. There is power in your creative thoughts and emotions, in how you focus your energy, in what you give your attention to.

You are a creative being made of love and light, and there are only layers or veils of forgetfulness that cause you to neglect this, that dim your power. Those layers are being removed now on your behalf, and even more so with your collaborative spirit, with your assistance, as you deliberately choose to awaken and remember.

Your intention is a powerful tool, and when you use your intention for the betterment of all, you are moving consciousness toward the unified whole. You are using your creative power to affect the "greater good," which includes your own good, your own well-being. In doing this, you call to you the aid and assistance of powers beyond the little you, the small self, and you grow in your ability to manifest your heart's deepest desires. You begin to work with the energies that create worlds.

When you work with the unified field, your creative power is limitless. When you seek to control others or manipulate them to get your way, from the lens of the small self, you may think *that* is power, but instead, you are holding yourself back, limiting or dimming your power. Why? Because you are cutting yourself off from the collaborative spirit, from the greater whole, pretending like competition or hierarchy is necessary for you to be in power. That is the old definition, the old way, the limited way. And if you choose to continue playing in those realms, you remain captive to the density from which those realms of consciousness are created.

Your heart has an intelligence of its own and is a force of power like no other. When you center yourself in your heart, you will access true power. You're less powerful when you're a slave to your mind-based illusions, which take center stage when your heart is closed. True power is not bestowed upon just anyone. You must be willing to remove yourself from the false hierarchical programming and beliefs born of competition, domination, and greed. None of these things exist within the purity of your higher heart. None of these things are in resonance with your soul.

Reclaiming Your Creational Power

There is no need to escape the programmed ego mind. Again, when you run from something, you make it *more* real, as if it's a monster that you must be afraid of. Your ego has no power or control over you, only the power or control you give it. Becoming intimately identified with the mind and believing every thought that surfaces is how we turn our power over. As we practice observing our thoughts with neutrality, we return to our soul's perspective.

The more you observe your limiting and fear-based thoughts, the easier it becomes to see them for what they are: falsified, illusory creations formed from a lack and separation consciousness. When you awaken to the realization that they are not your truth, they will begin to dissolve. These veils of illusion, which dimmed your light, will fall away, becoming thinner at first, thinner and thinner, and then they will evaporate. These heart walls you had built up when you were seeing through the eyes of separation will crumble, and you will remember once again that you are safe and loved and always will be.

Those beliefs that others can control you or have power over you or that you must control or have power over others, the belief that others can hurt you or vice versa, slowly reveal themselves as the nightmare of a separation-based illusion. You free yourself of this illusion by continually coming from the observer perspective, the reaction-less soul, the compassionate light being that you truly are and always have been. You open the floodgates for this surge of energy that flows through your being and out into your world. This is power surging through you, the divine frequency of love moving through your body as you return to presence.

Continue to open your heart and allow the thoughts based in separation to fall where they fall until they fall away for good. This is a moment-by-moment process. You will forget at times, but then you will remember. You will fall asleep and then wake up again, but you're not going backward. You're continually working your way up a spiral of evolution, of awakening. The ebbs and flows are all part of the experience, and you never need to beat yourself up or get down on yourself. As the observer, you do not judge; you do your best to continue focusing on that loving awareness, letting the rest fall away. Of course, intention can always be used to guide your path more powerfully, so if you commit to remembering, to stop forgetting, you will be greatly assisted in this undertaking.

As a conscious creator, you remember that what you focus on most prominently is what you are calling to you in your outer world reflections. And so you practice presence as if it were your full-time job. It is in this place of presence where all things are truly possible. It is where your soul-aligned guidance becomes crystal clear and you can activate your innate gifts and abilities from other existences that you had forgotten were inside of you. Within this space of consciousness, your heart's deepest desires can materialize in physical form. Here, you realize that your imagination is not make-believe but as real as you allow it to be. So breathing and birthing your potentials into reality becomes a natural process for you as a conscious creator. You no longer unconsciously react to fear-based constructs or take on painful perspectives. Now you breathe and bring forth higher light quotients, and you intentionally focus upon that which inspires, uplifts, and empowers your dream of unity.

CHAPTER 12—THE DREAM OF UNITY

Unity is a state of consciousness that you can tune in to and where you can reside full time as you relinquish limiting belief systems, raise your vibrational frequency, and ascend in consciousness. While this is an individual experience, it is also a collective experience, as greater numbers of the human collective unsubscribe from outdated belief systems born of fear and control and rise into this new vibration of exhalation. As individuals of the collective pull out of these belief systems, these old energetic systems or grids collapse, as they are only held together by a collective consensus. The physical structures and systems, such as systems of government, which were created from these unconscious beliefs, either dissolve (like you would dissolve a company) or transform and become birthed in their higher expression. In the years to come, we will see many systems of society, such as medical or healthcare, education, and financial institutions transform before our very eyes. Anything born of greed, control, suppression, disrespect, or lack of integrity will need to be restructured in alignment with the divine frequency of love, or it shall cease to be.

To some it may seem as though the world is ending, when in fact, it is going through one of the greatest transformations in human history, and all of Creation here is being rebirthed. We are being asked not to get too caught up in the drama and details of what's being broadcast on the news or happening "out there" and to trust that each individual being in consciousness has their own soul path to walk, which is divinely designed for their unique needs. As you stay your course, harmonizing and unifying everything from within and showing up as love with everyone you meet, eventually, a more heaven-like reality will become the out-picturing of your life's experience. This will be your unique dream of unity become manifest. New Earth is a name you can give this space of Unity Consciousness, this dream of unity. New Earth is the materialization of all that we truly desire and have been asking for as a human collective.

If you have ever sat in nature and felt the warm, loving embrace of Mother Earth, or looked into your lover's eyes and felt nothing but sheer gratitude for their very existence, then you have tuned in to the reality of New Earth. New Earth is a feeling, a remembrance, a frequency by which you tune in. It is not some place you get to by searching "out there." It is right here inside of you. You access this dimensional space by feeling into it, accepting it as something very real, very viable, and in doing this, you bring forth and support its physical manifestation. As you tune yourself like an instrument to the orchestration of divine harmonics, you create an energetic grid system alongside those who are equally accessing and playing in these Higher Consciousness realms. Together, we act as pillars of light that support and hold this grid, allowing the reality of New Earth to come alive.

To call forth a realm is to cease the need to skepticize, judge, or control how it may come into form. Our creative imagination is one of our God-given gifts and a tool for creation itself. As we create through intention in accordance with Divine Will, we can allow our creativity to blossom into something quite beautiful, and its expression will be sacred. Tune in to your higher heart and ask yourself, What would New Earth feel like, look like, sound, taste, or smell like if I were to step foot upon this magical realm? Let's paint the picture of a New Earth together, shall we?

The Dawning of New Earth

New Earth is Earth in a higher octave where things just look brighter, like they're in high definition, and sounds engulf you with their beauty. Clouds in the sky may appear fluffier or happier, while the saturation of colors is deeper and more prominent.

Here, it is natural for you to stop and smell the roses, as they speak to you telepathically. Here, you are not in a rush, as there is no place you would rather be than one with this present moment. Upon New Earth, you feel wild and free in your natural expression, and your Spirit moves your body toward whatever will nourish and uplift you. Here, you do not question the free-flowing line of energy, which draws you forward with effortless grace. You drink in the sun and you dance with the stars and you sing your soul's song with passion and exuberance.

Here, you can clearly see that your path is well-blessed, ripe with fun and freedoms once unimaginable. You play and create with the power of a thousand suns. You are free to express yourself joyfully, and laughter is a part of every conversation. You can communicate without words because you *feel* the one before you. Your heart is open and expansive, and love is the name of the game.

You flow with the winds, letting them carry you to new lands of exploration. Every breath you take opens you to new worlds of possibility. You remember your connection with All That Is, and the passion you carry within your heart guides your very existence. Not only are you moldable by your Spirit, but you embody your Spirit, your true essence, which is a bright, magnificent expression.

Perhaps one morning you wake up feeling so refreshed and rejuvenated that the cells in your body are dancing with orgasmic bliss and energy is pulsing through your being. As you brush your teeth, divine inspiration hits you. Today, you are inspired to write a song, which will put a smile on the faces of those who could use a little pep in their step. And so you spend your day playing with notes and creating lyrics. You are filled with great purpose and joy, and when you share your song with others, not only do you receive in return all the love you put into this soul expression of yours, but you also inspire others to put their creative abilities to work for the greater good.

Maybe the next day you become inspired to collaborate on a movie project with other beautiful beings who share a similar vision. Within this New Earth consciousness, there is no self-doubt or fear of survival as you know you are fully supported in what your heart calls you to each and every moment. What would it feel like to live in this state of consciousness? To create in unison with the flow of all Creation? Imagine each moment being centered in love and inspired by your deepest passions.

Within this New Earth consciousness, there is no time, only presence; and this presence showers you with presents unfathomable. You are nimble in your actions and intentional with your choices. You are fully available to those you are guided to play with, create with, dream with. Unconscious realities are but a distant thought now.

Your experiences are lived fully here as you are anchored in pure presence. As your energies align, harmonize, and unify, you become more and more powerful in your creative capacities. Imagine the ability to manifest your soul's desires instantaneously. As you align with the Divine Will, with your higher knowing, you are filled with joyous exuberance. You touch the hearts of others far and wide because you shine so brightly.

In this dream of unity, you no longer reach outside of yourself for anything, as you remember how to source from within. You do not strive or push, as now you act in accordance with your higher guidance, and you flow with the energies that create worlds. You fly high on the wings of loving awareness, illuminating your world in the most magical ways. Your world is therefore loving and kind, supportive and uplifting. You are trusting of those around you, and you trust your inner knowing with every ounce of your being.

You walk confidently and are constantly present-ed with beautiful gifts, as now you can see that all of life, all of existence, is a gift from God, from you to you. You perch high above the drama and details that used to trigger you and knock you off-kilter. Here, you know that all things can be made new, and you are empowered to continuously create from a unified perspective. Your soul is quenched, and you create in sync with the vibration of joy. You no longer stop yourself or sabotage your heart's deepest desires as you have now made all unconscious patterns conscious once again.

You are quick to step in and assist where needed, and you do so with great honor. You now have the capacity to hold space for others who are awakening to their own greater truths. You know yourself enough to know when it's time to rest and when it's time to act. You set loving and powerful boundaries with yourself and others, as you know that your boundaries activate others' highest alignment.

As you find your flow, your own rhythm with life, your dream becomes sparkly and delicious. You do not get caught up in "shoulds" or expectations that feel heavy or resistant, and when fear appears, you name it, move through it, and expand beyond it. Here, you are masterful at moving beyond limitation. Your heart guides you in this process. Having exercised compassion for all the parts of you that once felt scared, hurt, and alone, you return to a space of pure loving awareness.

You become literate in reading others' energy because you are so tuned in to your own energetic field. You are not motivated by quick fixes or band-aid remedies. Here, you are more interested in sustainable solutions that get to the root of whatever is not flowing freely. Because you care more about soul expansion than trying to keep things just the way they are or have been, you are greatly assisted in uplifting to your highest potential experiences.

Here, your highest potentials do not feel pressure-filled or stressful but more like exciting challenges or fun, new possibilities to play with. You do not take everything so seriously, as you know that being overly serious only causes drama and heartache. Play has become your new way. You play with your creations, realities, and your collaborators. You have fun with it all, and you laugh when things don't go quite as you had imagined.

An excitement and an enlivening feeling come with this new spontaneity that you've now surrendered to. When you kick up dust storms here and there, you aren't upset that your clothes have gotten dirty. Instead, you dance and play in the dirt until the rain cleanses you, like it always eventually does. The little things don't bother you anymore, as you no longer fear that things won't work out. You know with every fiber of your being that they will and always do. This faith opens you to possibilities beyond your wildest imagination, and you are constantly surprised, in the best possible ways, by what your universe has in store for you.

We rise in consciousness and collectively co-create New Earth through our intentions, our devotional practices, our creative imagination, our heart's dreams and desires, and the aligned or inspired actions that we are guided to flow with. As the old 3D matrixes and the realities they were formed from crumble and collapse, the new light grids and realities of New Earth are created and grow stronger with our loving awareness. We are tuning in to and aligning with what already exists as well as participating in the deliciousness of this New Earth co-creation. We are far from alone in this collective ascension process, and we are even being cheered on by beings in higher realms and collectives beyond this planet. Our graduation will be felt as this integration of light ripples out through the solar systems, universes, galaxies, and beyond.

The Flow of a Unified Consciousness

Life is here to support you every which way; all you have to do is allow it. Lean into it. If you can soften your defenses, surrender the nightmares, the fears, you open to that loving presence, which is what you innately are. You do not need to build yourself up; that is what the ego identity constructs were about. Instead, it is in relaxing, surrendering, and opening to who and what you have always been. This infinite intelligence, which you are one with, is here to guide your way. Trusting it is the key to unlocking your full potential, your greater expression.

You are not only worthy of embodying what we might call Christ Consciousness or a unified and unconditionally loving perspective, but it is your birthright, your destiny. Some might believe this can't be so: to sit like the gurus sit, to bring forth such deep wisdom, and to command your realities through the vibration of pure love, of pure joy. Yet, in essence, it is really just a practice of letting go of what no longer serves the greater good of all and merging with your Higher Consciousness perspectives. As you learn to do this successfully, you open new channels of energy, which energize and enliven you.

It is truly dazzling to witness someone who is in this flow, in what some call "flow state," as their logical thinking mind is out of the way and their natural instincts guide their every move. They are solely focused in the present moment, focused on the task at hand, and joyfully in sync with their wild and free spirit. It's as if nothing could stop them as they ride this momentous wave of high vibrational energy. This is a state of being that is always available to you and a space of consciousness where you can reside full-time as you dedicate yourself to this practice.

As you relax into a surrendered and receptive state, surrendered to your Spirit, you flow with all of life. When you pay special attention to the magic and synchronicities unfolding before you and through you, your life's dream becomes filled with miracles. You create in ways that dazzle, that ignite that creative force within you. Life is here for you, if only you can relax into this knowing.

A receptive, surrendered state is where you allow your divine destiny, your true calling, to emerge and reveal itself. The dreams of your Spirit are not far away, off in some distant lands; they are right here inside you. It is only in opening to them that they can and will become your new reality. This process of opening and expanding is a moment-by-moment practice of returning to love, of shifting back into alignment. No matter what circumstance presents itself, you always have the free will to take the higher road.

Stay open and present to each sign along your path, as your universe is always communicating with you. There are no coincidences, as every being, place, and situation has a message for you. If you are confronted with agitation or boredom, then perhaps it is time to grow beyond what you have known. Allow your feelings to be signposts without allowing them to rule your world.

Only you know what your heart truly wants to express and experience. Look within for that crystal-clear clarity. There is no need to let another's beliefs shape or create your future, as your divine destiny is *yours* to discover. Open your heart and allow the rivers of ancient wisdom to flow through you as you prepare for this journey you are embarking upon.

All the wisdom and resources and connections are within you. The dots are waiting to be connected. They are ready for you to click into place. The divine blueprint of your unique soul path is a hologram, which you can access as you step into and embody your Higher Consciousness, that truest, most expansive version of you. We turn the key to unlocking our true potential by making spaciousness within us and letting our light shine through.

Whatever is out of alignment, whatever no longer serves your greater expression, it is time to let that go. Your divine nature is not something that can be taken away from you, as it is what you are at the core of your very being. Allow yourself to be innocent and childlike once again. This is how you return to your roots.

Embodying a Receptive State of Grace

You are a beautiful expression of the Divine. What if you really felt this on a cellular level? What if you were to embody this? Not from an ego standpoint, but from a deep remembrance, a spark of knowingness.

You don't have to try to be anything—you just are. Here exists power and permission to relax and surrender the struggle, the fight to be something other than what you are, or the effort to be "some thing" at all. So throw your cares to the wind and relinquish your need to control, because the divine design of your life's unfolding will carry you, if you have the courage to let it.

Rather than trying to make it all happen, see if you can allow it to unfold. All you could ever want or need can and will occur, not by force or control, but through your grace and the grace of God Source Consciousness. Lean back and receive the support that is always here for you, always on standby, waiting for your allowance and permission. When we stop trying to go it alone and ask for what we need in a receptive and surrendered state, all that is required will be provided. And when we show up to meet our Spirit halfway, all that we truly want appears in the most magical and synchronistic of ways.

The Same Source We Blossom From

We are here to come together. When we support life, life supports us. It is a collaborative co-creation. When we feel nourished and full of life, we share that abundance of energy, of love, in exciting and uplifting ways. When we feel lost and in need of direction, or weighed down and in need of nourishment, we ask for support from God Source, our Higher Self, and our fellow light beings.

There is a peace that comes from knowing you are not alone. You do not have to look far to feel your connection to All That Is. There is a web that intrinsically links you to every being, every animal, every plant, every naturally occurring process. Much like our fungi networks, we are deeply rooted and connected to one another; we come from the very same Source. As much as we have believed that we are separate and alone, life continually reveals how truly loved, supported, and interconnected we are.

When we stop fighting this knowing, this remembrance, with painful stories, perspectives, and evidence, we allow ourselves to naturally blossom like our friendly fellow flowers do. The seedling of a flower starts its life in a dark and damp environment, yet its determination to grow is unhindered. It allows its life force energy to move it through the soil, past the rocks, and eventually, it breaks ground. The plant hadn't yet had an experience of the sun kissing its stem, but its keen instincts kept it growing anyway. At one time, this flower did not know it would eventually be surrounded by other unique and beautiful flowers just like it. It just kept growing, following that free-flowing line of energy, which propelled its expansion.

When that flower experiences its first petals blooming, it does not look around to compare the color or scent with its neighboring flowers. It's too enthralled with its own blossoming rapture, by how amazing this growth journey is turning out to be. This flower is not concerned with whether its petals are perfectly symmetrical or bending in the "right" ways. Instead, it is bathing in Divine Presence, expressing itself as the glory of God. This wildflower trusts that the rain will nourish it in divine right timing and the bees will carry on its lineage. Its only job is to continue growing into the sun. It is not with great effort but more of a surrender and allowance to what naturally wants to occur through it.

Your divine essence is as simple as this flower's. You can allow yourself to be nourished by the gifts of peace, love, and harmony, as they are available to you in all moments. Allow yourself to grow into this consciousness so that you exist here fully and freely.

Why Your Individuality Matters

Unity can sometimes be misunderstood to mean similarity, with the idea that to be unified as a collective we must all share the same viewpoints, think or feel the same about any given subject, or agree on one way to do things. This, however, is not why we signed up to be a part of a collective experience. It is our individuality and uniqueness that we bring forward, which makes any co-creative experience what it is or turns out to be. As we come together to work in collaboration with the Spirit of Creation, we each bring a unique ingredient to the table. Without your flour, for instance, the mixture may not allow the bread to rise.

Unity can be likened to harmonization rather than sameness. When you listen to an orchestra, you will hear all the various beautifully unique instruments, and while they all play different notes and tones, they are complimentary to one another. The music comes together to create a magnificent symphony of sound.

New Earth Ways, New Earth Priorities

In the nightmare of separation, we often find ourselves too busy or distracted to spend quality time with those we deeply care about. We might find ourselves prioritizing money, material possessions, or things that will build upon our success. Yet any time we place importance of things over our fellow beings of light, not only are we missing the point, but we are also operating from a programmed ego mind, and we will have to learn a hard lesson for ourselves. When someone is preparing for their transition into the afterlife, they aren't commonly filled with regrets regarding how much money they made or did not make; they're often regretful about losing touch with friends or family because they were so consumed with the busyness of their daily routines.

Inside the divine orchestration of Unity Consciousness, we will find ourselves spending more time with family, soul family, community, and friends, and this time and space will be cherished and prioritized. Here, we are at home with ourselves and at home with those around us because we have found home within our hearts. As a unified collective, councils, teams, groups, and families will assign creative roles to each individual rather than hierarchal structures where sovereignty is negated. Similar to how indigenous tribes gather in a circle to share wisdom traditions and stories, more and more people from all walks of life will gather around the hearth to collectively envision and create a more conscious, peaceful, and sustainable world.

As you embrace and embody the higher or more expansive versions of yourself, you learn to slow down and space out scheduled activities so that time is no longer an issue. Giving yourself this space is an act of love, and trusting that all will continue to work out for you is a practice. When time no longer dictates your choices, it is easier to make *conscious* choices. When you become so present in this moment, slowing everything down so you can make precise and coherent choices based in love, each of these choices acts as doorways or portals to greater expansion, greater awareness. This is how you free yourself from old, unconscious systems and structures that no longer serve you.

This spaciousness allows us to be more intentional about what we are investing our focus, energy, and money in. If you are investing in or engaging with corporations, for instance, that are operating from a place of greed or fear, then you are supporting that system's longevity and agreeing to its continuation. This anchors you to unconscious realities. If you begin to invest your energy in co-creating and participating in New Earth, which supports integrity, harmony, and collaboration for the greater good of all, then you are aligning yourself to a new world altogether.

Look at the intentions behind what you are investing your energy in. Are they pure? Are they answering the call for sustainable solutions? Or are they continuing the old, habitual ways of greed and waste? Where you spend your money matters. Where you place your focus dictates your outer world reflections.

In your life, look to see what you can share. Do you have an extra room in your house where someone with less material freedoms could stay for a while? Do you have extra money you could donate to a cause that aligns with your values? Do you have wisdom or expertise that could lift others out of pain and suffering? When we only do things to get money for our own wants and needs, we are re-contracting with a belief in separation. When we believe we need lots of material possessions to be happy or satisfied, we are sequestering ourselves to a world of superficiality. Yet when we look to see what is truly needed and how our innate gifts can answer that call, we become the trailblazers who bring unity consciousness into form.

As we come together to share with and support one another from a space of generosity, we strengthen that network of unity. Eventually, we will find that old systems like money no longer serve a purpose. There are already souls who exist outside of these structures, and opening your heart to share and collaborate within the unified field will magnetize you to these equally generous souls. You can learn to be generous without depleting your energy. When you share from that continually flowing Source within you, your re-sources never run dry. If you share from a place of "I" or "me," lack or need, you dam up that flow and exhaust yourself again and again.

The Invitation

As we move through our ascension process to express as a more unified consciousness, we are not only uplifting those aspects of us that had become frozen in fear and separation, but we are also activating and integrating our higher consciousness aspects. These aspects bring with them vast amounts of wisdom, gifts, and abilities. When we raise our vibration to meet these higher consciousness aspects, we are tasked with sustaining and maintaining this more expansive vibrational frequency. As we continue to do this, to be this, we are opening to quite literally embody all the higher consciousness aspects in existence. Whether or not you know the name of this more expansive consciousness or the group of beings that make up this consciousness as they come forth doesn't matter. What matters is that you can feel this new surge of energy moving through your being, through your body, and expressing in unison with you and as you.

The fullness of all that you are is waiting to be embodied by you, and yet you are never "late to the party," as all is unfolding in divinely perfect timing for your unique soul's journey. So stay present to the invitation to move into and flow with these more expansive and harmonious vibrations and take up the opportunity to reunite with all that you truly are.

Once you have activated and integrated enough light into each of your bodies of consciousness (mental, emotional, physical), you will reach a turning point where your soul fully steps forward with ease and directs your experience with pure presence in alignment with its Divine Will. Your ascension process will have brought you to fully merge with and embody your fifth-dimensional Higher Self version. Here, you will feel a deep sense of peace and "home" within.

There is no end, however, to the constant possibility and ever-unfolding choice of your soul's creative pursuits. This miraculous journey is something you choose as you surrender the burdens and detach yourself from anything that anchors you to a dense physical reality and as you choose to honor and embody your soul. This sacred process brings you into full alignment with your pure, divine essence, where you are reunited with the fullness and wholeness of All That Is. With every ego death comes a rebirth of your true expression, and with every breath comes the opportunity for new life to emerge.

The dream of unity exists within the purity of your higher heart. It is available to you as you tune in to it and merge with it. When you see your brothers and sisters in their highest light, as their true expression, and you hold a space of deep compassion and appreciation for all parts of them, you will feel the effects of Unity Consciousness inside of you and materializing around you. As you express the deepest reverence for all of life, you will open the door to your divine inheritance. Your sacred, intimate connection to yourself, to all beings, to all life forms, is strengthened by your ability to show up in love, as love, with respect and honor for All That Is. You are not only worthy of a heavenly experience of life in physical form, but it *is your divine birthright*, your greatest destiny. So dedicate yourself to allowing this divine destiny to be birthed through you, by you, as you, and awaken your heart to the union of all existences, all galaxies, all universes within you.

www.ingramcontent.com/pod-product-compliance
Lightning Source LLC
LaVergne TN
LVHW051836080426
835512LV00018B/2902